CANADA COOKS!

THE QUICK GOUR·MET

by

Eileen Dwillies

A Reader's World Book

Published by
Reader's World Books Ltd.
201-2525 Manitoba Street
Vancouver, B.C., Canada
V5Y 3A7

Produced by Opus Productions Inc.
1128 Homer Street
Vancouver, B.C., Canada
V6B 2X6

"Canada Cooks!" is a registered trademark of W.H. Smith Ltd.

© Copyright 1989 Opus Productions Inc.

Recipes © copyright 1989 Eileen Dwillies

Photography © 1989 Derik Murray

Canadian Cataloguing in Publication Data

Dwillies, Eileen.
    Canada cooks!: the quick gourmet

    1. Cookery.   I. Title.
TX715.D95 1989   641.5   C89-091409-5

Editor: Sheena Ashdown
Editorial Coordinator: Marthe Love
Production Manager: Orest Kinasevych
Designer: David Counsell
Food Stylist: Eileen Dwillies
Photography Coordinator: Frank Vena
Prop Stylist/Coordinator: Joanne Facchin
Photography Assistants: Perry Danforth, Grant Waddell
Electronic Publishing System Operator: Anne Groop
Food Stylist Assistant: Bill Wingate
Editorial Assistant: Wendy Darling

Opus Productions Inc. gratefully acknowledges the invaluable contributions of the
Vancouver companies who went above and beyond our expectations in supplying the
accessories pictured throughout this book: Arabesque, Atkinson Fine Imports, Birds of
Malden, Country Furniture, La Cache, Ming Wo, Panache, Pepitas Restaurant, Presents
of Mind, Tano's Brick Oven Pizza.

Produced exclusively on the IBM Personal Publishing System
and IBM PS/2 Personal Systems.

Front Cover Photo: Grilled Salmon

Printed in Canada by Friesen Printers

CONTENTS

ACKNOWLEDGEMENTS

Many thanks to Paul, Janet, Diane and son-in-law Jim, for their discriminating tastes and thoughtful advice. Thanks to my dear friends who, again and again, sat down to "test" food, and who shared their opinions and recipes freely over the years.

Thanks also to Derik Murray, for the beautiful photographs in this book, and to the staff at Opus Productions, for their patience and guidance.

INTRODUCTION

In THE QUICK GOURMET, I have presented a selection of innovative recipes for two. Some can be prepared in twenty minutes, while others require a little more time. All are aimed at those with busy lifestyles, who are cooking for two—or just themselves.

The recipes range from appetizers to desserts, from stir-fried dishes to oven-baked meals. I've included dishes of ethnic origin adapted for Canadian tastes. Many refer to other recipes in the book to complement them and build a full meal's menu.

All these recipes use fresh, wonderful ingredients readily available in local supermarkets. Some are made from scratch and some use prepared stocks and sauces available in specialty markets. The focus is on delicious taste and quick preparation—just for two!

If I have a culinary motto, it is "simple, yet elegant". My forté is developing ideas into recipes that exemplify this motto. As my lifestyle has changed over the past few years, I have relied more on stocks and sauces from specialty shops. I find that I put more emphasis on grilled and sautéed dishes in my daily cooking. Creative cooking has become a luxury I look forward to on weekends.

As I visit restaurants around the city and country, I have seen great changes. The new menus feature heartier fare and simpler recipes, which call for fresh local ingredients and less fussy foods. They are cutting back on exotic ingredients and heavily decorated presentations.

I like great flavours and enjoy the challenge of using herbs and spices with a deft touch—or with gusto when appropriate! My preferred herbs are oregano, thyme, savoury, tarragon, basil and, always, parsley. Among the spices, I like cayenne, nutmeg, pepper, pepper and more pepper.

Enthusiasm for eating and good food is the beginning point for anyone starting in the kitchen. A few good tools also make life easier. My favourites are a 10" (25 cm) Castoflan pan by Le Crueset, a 2 qt. (2 L) copper (nickel-lined) saucepan, a 9" (22 cm) Henckels chef's knife and an 8" (20 cm) Henckels bread knife.

All the recipes in this book have been tested many times at my dining room table or in my cooking school. Feel free to taste and adjust according to your preferences. Although I haven't specified it, I used unsalted butter at all times. The butter is fresher and you don't have adjust the recipe for salt.

Wonderful food. Simple preparation. Careful choice of ingredients. Good presentation. That sums up my philosophy!

Bon appetit!

APPETIZERS

A dazzling beginning to a wonderful evening, fancy finger food complements easy conversation. But it is often the most difficult food to create.
I have given some simple outlines as basic ideas. Use them to build
upon. Served individually or altogether, they will make your reputation!

ANTIPASTO

A small antipasto platter is a great way to stave off hunger pangs while dinner is being prepared. Some suggested items include a tin of imported anchovies, pickled Italian peppers, stuffed green olives or tuna Italian style. Keep some of these canned items ready on your shelf for unexpected guests. Serve with a glass of crisp white wine.

1/2 lb. (250 g)	thinly sliced salami
1- 375 mL can	ripe olives
1/2 lb. (250 g)	provolone cheese, sliced
1 - 2- 50 g cans	small imported sardines
	Ham-Filled Mushroom Caps, page 9
	Marinated Artichokes, page 8

MARINATED ARTICHOKES

1- 14 oz. (398 mL) can	artichokes
3 tbsp. (45 mL)	lemon juice
2 tbsp. (30 mL)	olive oil
1	clove garlic, chopped

Cut artichokes into small pieces. Add lemon juice, oil and garlic. Mix well and place in refrigerator for 1 day or more.

HAM-FILLED MUSHROOM CAPS

1/2 lb. (250 g)	large mushrooms
	olive oil
2 tbsp. (30 mL)	minced onions
1	clove garlic
4 tbsp. (60 mL)	finely chopped ham
4 tbsp. (60 mL)	soft fine bread crumbs
1 tbsp. (15 mL)	Parmesan cheese
1	egg
1 tbsp. (15 mL)	chopped fresh parsley
1 tsp. (5 mL)	chopped fresh oregano
1/2 tsp. (2 mL)	salt
	fresh pepper

Remove mushroom stems from mushrooms. Chop enough stems to measure 4 tbsp. (60 mL) and set aside. Heat 2 tbsp. (30 mL) oil in a skillet. Add mushroom caps and toss. Remove caps from pan and reserve.

To the skillet, add the chopped mushroom stems, onions and garlic. Cook 10 minutes until mixture is almost a pulp. Remove from heat. Add remaining ingredients.

Place stuffing mixture in mushroom caps. Arrange in baking dish. Bake at 350° F (180° C) for 30 minutes, or until heated through and lightly browned.

CLASSIC ESCARGOT

I prefer the snails from France for this dish because they seem more tender.
Serve this dish with lots of fresh baguette bread for sopping up the juices.
Replace the snails with smoked mussels and the snail shells with mushroom
caps if you like. **Makes 24**.

24	snail shells
2- 4 1/2 oz. (125 g) cans	imported snails
2 tbsp. (30 mL)	dry white wine
1	shallot, finely sliced
1	clove garlic, thinly sliced
6	thin slices of carrot
dash	thyme
	small piece of bay leaf
	pinch of parsley
	salt and pepper

Wash the shells in hot water and drain well. Cool.

Empty the snails with their liquid into a pot. Add the remaining ingredients. Bring to a boil. Cover and simmer for 10 minutes. Let cool and drain.

While cooking the above, make the snail butter for stuffing the snail shells as follows.

3/4 cup (175 mL)	unsalted butter, softened
4 tbsp. (60 mL)	finely chopped parsley
2 tbsp. (30 mL)	fine dry crumbs
1 tbsp. (15 mL)	finely chopped garlic
1 tbsp. (15 mL)	finely chopped shallots
	salt and pepper

Cream all of the above ingredients together.

When the snails have cooled, spoon about 1/2 tsp. (2 mL) of the snail butter into each shell, pushing it down with your fingers. Add 1 snail to each shell, also pushing it in. Spoon equal portions of the remaining snail butter into each shell, filling completely. Smooth off the butter at the opening of each shell.This dish may be made in advance to this point, then refrigerated or frozen. Any leftover butter is great on hot bread.

To prepare the snails, heat the oven to 500° F (260° C). Arrange the snails in the traditional snail dishes or place them on coarse salt to hold them upright on ovenproof serving plates. Bake for 5 minutes, or until sizzling hot. Serve immediately.

MUSHROOMS IN PARCHMENT

A delightful beginning to any meal, this dish can be made for any number of people. Chanterelle, shiitake or oyster mushrooms can be used for a change of pace. Serve as a light first course.

8 oz. (250 g)	plump, fresh mushrooms
2 tbsp. (30 mL)	finely chopped parsley
	freshly ground pepper
1	large clove garlic, finely chopped
2 tbsp. (30 mL)	fine bread crumbs
2 tbsp. (30 mL)	olive oil
	juice of 1/2 lemon
	parchment paper
	oil *or* butter
2	thin slices of lemon for garnish

If using wild mushrooms, check carefully for sand and dirt. Cut the mushrooms into fairly thick slices and place in a bowl. Add all the remaining ingredients except the lemon slices, parchment and oil. Toss well.

Cut the parchment into 2 rectangles 12" x 8" (30 cm x 20 cm). Brush with oil or butter. Divide the mushroom mixture between the 2 pieces of parchment. Fold each in half and seal by tightly folding the edges. Brush the outsides with more oil or butter.

Place the parchment packages on a baking sheet. Bake at 350° F (180° C) for about 10–15 minutes, or until they puff slightly and are golden. Place on serving plates and tear open. Garnish with lemon slices.

HAM PUFFS

The delicious puff is made from Pâte au Choux pastry, one of the quickest and easiest pastries to prepare. When you know how to make it, you can make Gougere and Paris Brest as well as eclairs and cream puffs! Serve this dish in small slices for an appetizer or large wedges for a light first course.

Pastry

1/2 cup (125 mL)	butter, coarsely chopped
1 cup (250 mL)	water
1 cup (250 mL)	white all purpose flour
1 tsp. (5 mL)	salt
4	large eggs

Heat the butter and water to boiling in a heavy saucepan. Leave on the heat only until butter melts, then remove immediately. Add all the flour and salt. Beat vigorously with a wooden spoon. Return to low heat 1–2 minutes. Beat until the paste leaves the sides of the pan and forms a ball, and a light film shows on the bottom of the pan, about 2 minutes.

Remove from heat. Add eggs, 1 at a time, beating well after each addition. (A food processor is good for this step.) Beat until paste is smooth and glossy, and drops in clumps from the spoon. It may not be necessary to add all of the fourth egg.

For a savoury pastry, add 2 oz. (60 g) diced cheddar cheese and a dash of salt and pepper.

On two well-greased ovenproof plates or pottery dishes (or one 10" [25.5 cm] quiche dish), arrange the pastry around the sides, leaving a hollow in the centre. Set aside.

Filling

2 tbsp. (30 mL)	butter
1	medium onion, chopped
2	large mushrooms, sliced
1 - 2 tbsp. (15 - 30 mL)	white all purpose flour
1 cup (250 mL)	chicken broth
2	medium tomatoes, seeded and chopped
4 - 6 oz. (125 - 180 g)	shredded Black Forest ham
1 tbsp. (15 mL)	grated Parmesan cheese
1 tbsp. (15 mL)	fine dry bread crumbs
1 tbsp. (15 mL)	chopped fresh parsley

Melt the butter in a medium skillet. Add the onion. Sauté for several minutes. Add the mushrooms and cook briefly. Sprinkle in the flour and stir. Pour in the broth and simmer for about 5 minutes. Remove from heat. Stir in the tomatoes and ham.

Spoon the filling into the centre of the puff. Mix together the Parmesan cheese and crumbs. Sprinkle over the ham mixture. Bake at 425° F (220° C) for 30–35 minutes, or until puff is very well browned. Remove from oven and sprinkle with chopped parsley.

VEGETABLE DIP

Slice vegetables of your choice and arrange them on a lettuce-lined platter around a bowl of this refreshing dip.

1/2 cup (125 mL)	mayonnaise
4 tbsp. (60 mL)	sour cream
1 tbsp. (15 mL)	chopped parsley
1 tsp. (5 mL)	grated onion
1 tsp. (5 mL)	lemon juice
1/2 tsp. (2 mL)	Worcestershire sauce
1/2 tsp. (2 mL)	crushed mixed dried herbs
pinch	each, salt and curry powder

Mix all the ingredients together thoroughly. Chill overnight.

TAPENADE DIP

Serve this classic Greek dip with fresh vegetables. It is particularly good with raw parsnip, zucchini, carrots and jicama. Try quarters of pita bread along with the vegetables. **Makes 1 1/2 cups (375 mL).**

4 tbsp. (60 mL)	loosely packed parsley
2 tbsp. (30 mL)	drained capers
5	anchovy fillets, rinsed and dried
6	pitted ripe olives
1	peeled clove of garlic
	juice of 1/2 lemon
1	slice of white bread, crumbled
pinch	freshly ground black pepper
1	large egg
1 cup (250 mL)	olive oil

Place all the ingredients, except the egg and oil, in the bowl of a food processor. Process briefly. Stop and scrape the bowl down. Continue processing and scraping until mixture is a smooth thick paste. Break the egg into the bowl and process for several seconds.

With the motor running, drizzle the oil down the feed tube in a fine stream. Continue processing for 10 more seconds to incorporate all the oil.

Store in the refrigerator. Bring to room temperature before serving. The dip will keep for about 5 days.

SOUPS

Soup is the real first course, above and beyond the appetizer. And it is my favorite starter. Chilled, warm, creamed or clear, it's a wonderful way to start dinner.

DOUBLE MUSHROOM SOUP

This delicious creamed soup goes well with a beef entrée. It is best served soon after it is made. For a more intense flavour, use the dried mushrooms in the stock.

2 tbsp. (30 mL)	butter
1	small onion, chopped
1	clove garlic, minced
4 oz. (125 g)	fresh mushrooms, chopped *or*
1 oz. (30 g)	dried mushrooms
	(If you use dried mushrooms, soak them first in warm water for about 5 minutes. Rinse to remove any sand. Strain the liquid and use with the chicken stock. Chop mushrooms.)
1 cup (250 mL)	chicken stock *or* canned broth
1	bay leaf
pinch	salt
	freshly ground pepper
4	whole fresh mushrooms
4 tbsp. (60 mL)	cream
1 tbsp. (15 mL)	Madeira *or* sherry
	parsley for garnish

In a medium saucepan, melt the butter. Sauté the onion until tender. Add the garlic and cook another minute. Stir in the mushrooms. Add the chicken stock, bay leaf, salt and pepper. Bring to a boil. Reduce the heat and simmer 15–20 minutes. Discard the bay leaf.

Cool the soup slightly. Purée in a blender. The dish may be made ahead to this point and frozen, if desired. Keep at room temperature for use within a few hours. Refrigerate for use the next day.

Just before serving, slice the fresh whole mushrooms. Return the soup to the saucepan and stir in the cream. Reheat gently, but do not boil. Taste and adjust for seasonings. Add the sliced mushrooms and the Madeira. Garnish with parsley.

Opposite: Classic Escargot

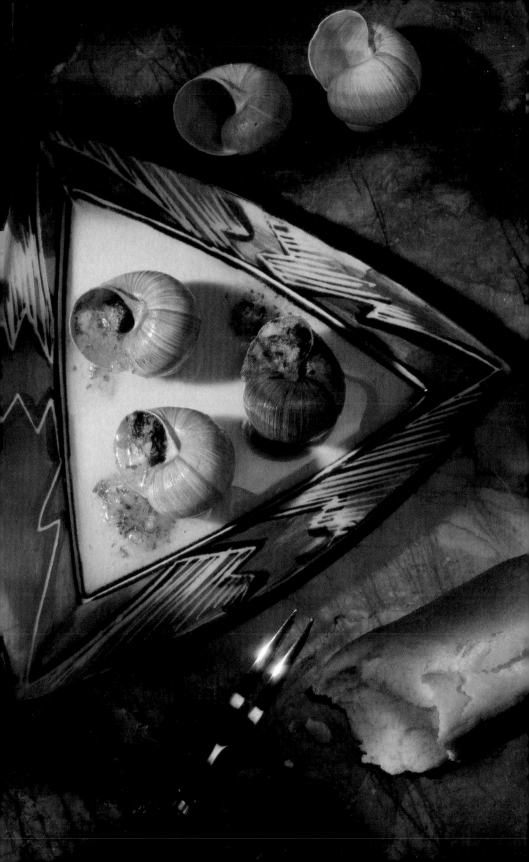

CREAM OF BROCCOLI SOUP

Creamy and smooth, this pale green soup makes a good first course. The recipe doubles and freezes well.

2 tbsp. (30 mL)	butter
1	small onion, sliced
1	small potato, peeled and sliced
1 cup (250 mL)	coarsely chopped broccoli
1 1/2 cups (375 mL)	chicken stock *or* canned broth
	salt and pepper to taste
1/2 cup (125 mL)	whipping cream

Melt butter in large saucepan. Do not let it brown. Add vegetables. Cover with parchment or waxed paper and lid. Simmer gently until vegetables are soft but not brown. (This is called "sweating the vegetables".)

Remove parchment. Add the chicken stock. Bring to a boil and simmer until vegetables are well cooked. Cool slightly.

Purée the mixture in a blender until smooth or the desired texture. Pour back into the cleaned saucepan. Season with salt and pepper (a dash of cayenne or tabasco is nice too). Add the whipping cream and bring to a simmer. Do not let the mixture boil or cream will curdle.

Serve hot. If you wish to serve cold, let cool and refrigerate. Serve with a topping of sour cream.

To prepare frozen soup, thaw and put through the blender if the cream has separated.

FRESH CORN SOUP

Make this soup in mid-August, when corn is at its best. One average-sized cob yields about 1/2 cup (125 mL) kernels.

2 tbsp. (30 mL)	butter
1	small onion, chopped
1/2	green bell pepper, finely chopped
1 cup (250 mL)	milk
1 tbsp. (15 mL)	chopped parsley
1 tbsp. (15 mL)	chopped fresh savoury
pinch	salt
	freshly ground pepper to taste
1 cup (250 mL)	corn kernels
1/2 cup (125 mL)	whipping cream
2 tbsp. (30 mL)	corn kernels for garnish

In a medium saucepan, melt the butter. Sauté the onion and pepper until tender. Add the milk, parsley, savoury, salt, pepper and corn. Bring to a boil. Reduce heat and simmer about 10 minutes.

Cool the soup slightly. Purée in a blender (remember that hot liquids tend to pop the blender lid!). Return the puréed mixture to the saucepan and reheat to simmer.

Add the cream. Taste and adjust for seasonings. Serve hot with a spoonful of the reserved whole corn kernels.

GAZPACHO

This hot weather soup from Spain is delicious and healthy. This recipe makes enough for eight people. It will keep, refrigerated, for one week to ten days.

5	medium tomatoes, seeded and chopped
1	medium green bell pepper
1	clove garlic, crushed
1	mild onion, peeled and thinly sliced
1	English cucumber, peeled, seeded and chopped
1/2 cup (125 mL)	chopped mixed herbs, such as chives, parsley, basil, oregano, chervil, tarragon
1/2 cup (125 mL)	good quality olive oil
3 tbsp. (45 mL)	lemon juice
1- 290 mL bottle	chili sauce
1 cup (250 mL)	water
	parsley *or* lemon slices for garnish

Place the tomatoes, pepper, garlic, onion and cucumber in a blender or food processor. Blend until finely chopped. Transfer to a large bowl.

Mix together the herbs, olive oil, lemon juice and chili sauce. Add to the chopped vegetables.

Chill for 4 hours or more. If the soup becomes too thick, add up to 1 cup (250 mL) of water. Garnish with parsley or lemon slices.

NUT AND CURRY SOUP

Curry-scented with a rich nutty flavour, this soup will earn you raves!

2 tbsp. (30 mL)	butter
1	small onion, chopped
1	green apple, peeled, cored and chopped
1	clove garlic, minced
1 tsp. (5 mL)	curry powder, or to taste
pinch	salt
	freshly ground pepper
2 cups (500 mL)	chicken stock *or* canned broth
1/2 cup (125 mL)	Nut Butter, recipe follows

In a medium saucepan, melt the butter. Sauté the onion and apple until tender. Add the garlic, curry powder, salt and pepper. Cook 2–3 minutes more. Add chicken stock and simmer for 10 minutes. Cool slightly.

Purée soup in a blender. Gradually add the Nut Butter. The soup may be prepared ahead to this point and frozen. To prepare frozen soup for serving, reheat but do not boil.

Nut Butter

1 cup (250 mL)	toasted nuts, such as cashews, almonds, peanuts or hazelnuts, with skins removed
2 - 3 tsp. (10 - 15 mL)	vegetable oil

Grind the nuts in a food processor or blender until coarse in texture. With the food processor running, add the oil. Continue to process until smooth.

VICHYSSOISE

Served cold, this soup is called Vichyssoise. Served hot, it's Cream of Potato! Purée well because it needs to be very smooth.

3	leeks, white part only
1	large potato, peeled and sliced
3 tbsp. (45 mL)	butter
1 cup (250 mL)	chicken stock *or* canned broth
	salt
1/2 cup (125 mL)	half and half cream
	nutmeg and pepper to taste
	chopped chives

Slice the leeks and potatoes. Cook in butter until soft but not brown. Add stock and a little salt. Cook, covered, until vegetables are very tender. Cool.

Purée in blender. Add cream. Season to taste with nutmeg, salt and pepper. Simmer 2–3 minutes, but do not allow to boil. Cool and chill thoroughly.

Serve cold garnished with a sprinkling of chives.

SALADS

I like to eat my salad after the main dish. It is said to help digest food and prepare your stomach for the most important course—dessert! The salads here cover the gamut from light, between-course dishes to luncheons to main dishes. Although salads have new importance, the key to their success is simplicity: wonderful dressings over beautiful greens. Summer salads are the best salads of all. Everything is at the peak of its flavour and only needs a splash of vinaigrette and a sprinkle of herbs to achieve perfection.

CHICKEN SALAD

Serve Classic Escargot as the first course with this delicious salad for a dinner out of the ordinary.

1	whole chicken breast, cooked, skinned, boned and diced
1/2 cup (125 mL)	Green Goddess Dressing, page 46
1/2 lb. (250 g)	bacon slices, chopped
1	stalk celery, finely diced
1 cup (250 mL)	finely chopped romaine
1 cup (250 mL)	chopped watercress
	salt and pepper

In a medium bowl, mix the prepared chicken with the dressing. Chill.

Sauté bacon until very crisp. Drain well and cool. Set aside. Add the celery, romaine and watercress to chicken. Mix well and season to taste with salt and pepper. Spoon onto chilled serving plates. Top with bacon and serve.

CHICKEN AND CABBAGE SALAD

Serve Ham Puffs to start this meal of sweet and sour chicken salad with eggs. Any vinaigrette can be used in this salad, but Sweet and Sour Vinaigrette gives an extra-special taste.

8 slices	grilled, poached or roasted poultry
1	medium red onion, finely chopped
	buckwheat noodles, vermicelli *or* sautéed shredded red cabbage
	Sweet and Sour Vinaigrette, page 44
4	hard-boiled eggs
	toasted sesame seeds

Slice the poultry into thin rounds or shred into strips. Toss with the onions. Arrange over the cooked noodles, vermicelli or cabbage. Spoon over the dressing. Garnish with slices of hard-boiled egg and sprinkle with sesame seeds.

As a variation, mix the chicken and onions in the dressing. Let stand for 1/2 hour. Place over the cabbage and garnish with egg slices and sesame seeds.

CHUNKY CHICKEN SALAD

Serve this dish for supper on a hot summer's evening along with Ham-Filled Mushroom Caps.

2 tbsp. (30 mL)	white wine vinegar
2 tbsp. (30 mL)	oil
pinch	each, salt, white pepper and dried tarragon
1 1/2 cups (375 mL)	cooked chicken, cut in chunks
4 - 5	whole fresh mushrooms, thinly sliced
1	small green bell pepper, thinly sliced
1	medium tomato, cut in wedges
	a few slices of cucumber
	lettuce *or* other salad greens
1	hard-cooked egg yolk, sieved or finely chopped

In a medium bowl, combine the wine vinegar, oil and seasonings. Toss in the chicken, mushrooms and pepper. Cover tightly. Marinate in the refrigerator for at least 1 hour.

Add tomatoes and cucumber. Toss and spoon on lettuce-lined plates. Garnish with egg yolk.

COCKTAIL DE LA MER DU NORD

This recipe calls for shrimp, crab and barbequed salmon, which are served on crisp lettuce and garnished with a slice of hard-cooked egg and caviar. **Serves 4–6**.

1/2	iceberg lettuce
2 oz. (60 g)	fresh cooked shrimp, chilled
2 oz. (60 g)	fresh cooked crab meat, chilled
2 oz. (60 g)	barbecued salmon, chilled
2	large raw mushrooms
	Oil and Vinegar Dressing, page 47
1	hard-cooked egg, sliced
1- 2 oz. (57 g) jar	black caviar (lumpfish)
2	lemon wedges
2	sprigs of parsley

Shred lettuce and place on 2 small glass plates. On the lettuce, arrange clusters of shrimp, crab meat, salmon and sliced mushrooms. Sprinkle with a few spoonfuls of the dressing. Place a slice of egg in the centre of each. Top with a small spoonful of caviar. Garnish with a lemon wedge and parsley sprig.

DEVILLED CRAB SALAD

Serve this salad as a light supper or with a warm bowl of soup.

1 lb. (500 g)	fresh crab meat
1 cup (250 mL)	cracker crumbs, unsalted
2	stalks celery, finely diced
4 tbsp. (60 mL)	chopped onion
4 tbsp. (60 mL)	melted butter
4 tbsp. (60 mL)	half and half cream
1 tsp. (5 mL)	dry mustard
1/2 tsp. (2 mL)	salt
dash	cayenne pepper
2 tbsp. (30 mL)	chopped parsley
1 tbsp. (15 mL)	chopped green bell pepper
dash	hot pepper sauce

Pick over the crab meat to check for shells. Place in a medium bowl. Lightly crumble the crackers with your hands. Combine the crab with the crumbs. Moisten the celery and onion with the butter and cream. Add to crab mixture. Season with the mustard, salt, cayenne, parsley, green pepper and hot pepper sauce. Mix thoroughly.

Pile into shells or a casserole. Bake at 350° F (180° C) until heated through. Serve immediately.

HOT SPINACH SALAD

This salad is wonderful with a pasta such as Fettucine Alla Carbonara.

1	large peeled clove of garlic
4 oz. (125 g)	ham, cut into 4 pieces
2 tbsp. (30 mL)	olive oil
4 tbsp. (60 mL)	pine nuts
4 tbsp. (60 mL)	blanched slivered almonds
1/2 lb. (250 g)	fresh spinach, washed, dried and ripped into bite-sized pieces
	salt

Into a running food processor, drop garlic through feed tube. Process until finely minced. Remove and reserve. Add ham to bowl. Process with on/off motion until finely diced. Remove and reserve.

In a large skillet, heat olive oil over moderate heat. Add minced garlic. Cook 1 minute (do not burn). Add the pine nuts and almonds to hot oil. Cook 2–3 minutes until nuts are lightly browned. Add spinach leaves, ham and salt. Toss until all ingredients are mixed and heated thoroughly. Serve immediately.

CARROT SALAD IN LETTUCE CUPS

The flavour of this salad improves with time, so it's best made a day or two ahead.

2	medium carrots, peeled and cut into thin julienne strips about 2" (5 cm) long
1 tbsp. (30 mL)	fresh lemon juice
1/2 cup (125 mL)	loosely packed parsley leaves, finely chopped
1	hard-cooked egg, peeled and coarsely chopped
1 - 2	green onions, coarsely chopped
1	small dill pickle, coarsely chopped
1 tbsp. (15 mL)	capers, drained
1 tbsp. (15 mL)	Dijon mustard, or to taste
1 tsp. (5 mL)	chopped fresh tarragon *or* 1/2 tsp. (2 mL) dried tarragon
4 tbsp. (60 mL)	Homemade Mayonnaise, page 49
	lettuce leaves
	parsley sprigs

Place the carrots in a medium bowl. Sprinkle with lemon juice and toss to coat. Add 4 tbsp. (60 mL) of the chopped parsley. Set the remainder aside for the mayonnaise.

Mix together the eggs, onion, dill pickle, capers, Dijon mustard and tarragon. Add the reserved parsley. Stir in the mayonnaise. Season to taste. Stir into the carrot mixture. Chill until serving time.

When ready to serve, arrange lettuce leaves on a chilled platter. Place carrot mixture in centre of each. Garnish with a whole sprig of parsley.

COTTAGE CHEESE AND TOMATO SALAD

Serve with fresh hot rolls and glasses of cider to make this salad a good luncheon dish.

1 cup (250 mL)	cream-style cottage cheese
2 tbsp. (30 mL)	chopped green bell pepper
2 tbsp. (30 mL)	finely shredded carrot
2 tbsp. (30 mL)	finely chopped onion
	ground pepper
pinch	cayenne pepper
4 tbsp. (60 mL)	salad dressing *or* mayonnaise
	lettuce
	tomato wedges *or* cherry tomatoes

In a medium bowl, combine cottage cheese, green pepper, carrot and onion. Add peppers to taste. Stir in salad dressing. Cover and chill. Serve chilled on individual lettuce-lined plates. Garnish with tomatoes.

NOUVELLE POTATO SALAD

Serve Mushrooms In Parchment with these tangy mustard potatoes to make a great meal. Depending on the size of the potatoes, plan on serving two per person when making this recipe as a salad course.

2 tbsp. (30 mL)	mustard
1/2 cup (125 mL)	water
4	small new potatoes, peeled and cut into 1" (2.5 cm) cubes
	lettuce for garnish

Place the mustard and water in a medium saucepan. Bring to a boil. Add the potato pieces. Stir well. Cook until potatoes are tender, stirring often, about 10 minutes. Serve at once, or at room temperature, on a lettuce leaf.

PASTA SALAD

Soup and a salad are a great combination—in this case, Vichyssoise and Pasta Salad! Fusilla pasta, sometimes called rigatoni, are tiny colourful coils often found in the bulk foods section.

1 1/2 cups (375 mL)	dried fusilla pasta *or* small macaroni
5 or 6	radishes, sliced
3 or 4	green onions, sliced
	Balsamic Vinaigrette, page 45
	lettuce

Cook the pasta or macaroni until tender, about 20 minutes. Toss with radishes, green onions and a few spoonfuls of Vinaigrette. Serve on a lettuce leaf, warm or at room temperature. Pass the extra dressing.

Opposite: Salata (Greek Salad).

TUNA-APPLE SALAD

This is a hearty salad for lunch or a light supper.

1 cup (250 mL)	shredded cabbage
1- 7 oz. (198 g) can	chunk tuna, drained
4 tbsp. (60 mL)	shredded cheddar cheese
4 tbsp. (60 mL)	thinly sliced celery
6 tbsp. (90 mL)	mayonnaise
1 tbsp. (15 mL)	lemon juice
1 tsp. (5 mL)	oil
pinch	dry mustard
	salt and pepper
1	medium apple, cored and chopped

In a medium bowl, combine cabbage, tuna, cheese and celery. Chill well.

Blend together the mayonnaise, lemon juice, oil and mustard. Taste for seasonings. Chill.

To serve, toss dressing mixture with tuna mixture. Stir in apples.

SALATA (Greek Salad)

This is a cool and refreshing salad to serve before a spicy Calzone or Quick and Easy Pizza.

1	firm ripe tomatoes, cut into wedges
1/2	small English cucumber, scored and cut into chunks
2	medium green onions with tops, chopped, *or* mild onion chunks
	kalamata olives
2 - 3 tbsp. (30 - 45 mL)	Dilled Oil and Vinegar Dressing, page 47
2 tbsp. (30 mL)	feta cheese
	freshly ground pepper
	oregano

Combine all the vegetables in a medium salad bowl. Pour on a little dressing and mix well. Crumble feta cheese on top. Season with the pepper and oregano.

TOMATO AND EGG SALAD WITH BOILED DRESSING

This salad is made with a delicious dressing much like mayonnaise in texture but without the oil. It's an elegant dish to serve as a first course for company.
Serves 4.

4	large tomatoes
4	large eggs
	butter lettuce
	salt and pepper to taste
	Boiled Dressing, recipe follows
	pimento, olives *or* pickles, finely chopped

Plunge the tomatoes into boiling water for 10 seconds. Cool under cold running water and peel off the skins. Chill thoroughly. Hard cook the eggs by placing them in cold water in a saucepan and bringing them to a boil. Cover and let stand for 20 minutes. Cool under cold water and refrigerate.

At serving time, arrange the lettuce leaves on a large platter. Cut the tomatoes in half and place on the lettuce, cut side up. Cut the hard boiled eggs in half lengthwise. Sprinkle with salt and pepper. Place cut side down on the tomato half. Spoon the boiled dressing carefully over the top of the egg. Sprinkle on a little of the chopped pimento.

Boiled Dressing

1 tbsp. (15 mL)	white all purpose flour
1 1/2 tsp. (7 mL)	sugar
2 tsp. (10 mL)	salt, or to taste
2	egg yolks, beaten
3 tbsp. (45 mL)	butter, melted
3/4 cup (175 mL)	milk
4 tbsp. (60 mL)	mild vinegar
	pepper and dried tarragon to taste

Place all the ingredients, except the pepper and tarragon, in a heavy saucepan or in the top of a double boiler. Stir well. Cook slowly on medium heat or over hot water, whisking constantly, until the mixture coats the back of a wooden spoon. Strain into a small bowl. Cool. Taste and adjust for seasonings. Add white pepper and chopped or dried tarragon, if desired. Keep refrigerated.

WARM BEAN SALAD

Warm white beans, topped with marinated winter vegetables, make a comforting dish for cold days.

3/4 cup (175 mL)	small white beans
	water
1/2 cup (125 mL)	chicken stock *or* canned broth
1	small onion, finely chopped
2 tbsp. (30 mL)	finely chopped parsley
1 tbsp. (15 mL)	finely chopped fresh oregano
	freshly ground pepper
	Vinaigrette, page 44
2	carrots, peeled and sliced
1/2	small turnip, peeled and sliced
	a few small cauliflower florets
1	medium tomato, cut in small chunks
	lettuce *or* romaine leaf

Cover beans with 2" (5 cm) of water and let stand overnight. Drain. Place in a saucepan and cover with 2" (5 cm) fresh water. Bring to a boil. Simmer, uncovered, until barely tender. Add the chicken broth, onion, parsley and oregano. Stir well. Bring to a boil. Cook, uncovered, until the liquid has just evaporated. Spoon into a bowl to cool. Season with pepper to taste. Stir in 2 tbsp. (30 mL) of the Vinaigrette.

Cook the carrots, turnip and cauliflower until tender crisp. Place in a bowl. Add the tomato. While still warm, toss with the Vinaigrette to coat.

When ready to serve, gently reheat the beans. Place on a leaf of lettuce and top with the vegetables. Pass the extra dressing.

RICE MEDLEY

This recipe can be doubled, but to keep the salad light, don't increase the amount of barley.

4 tbsp. (60 mL)	raw rice
4 tbsp. (60 mL)	barley
4 tbsp. (60 mL)	raisins
4 tbsp. (60 mL)	whole almonds, toasted and coarsely chopped
1 tbsp. (15 mL)	parsley, finely chopped
	Vinaigrette, page 44
	lettuce *or* romaine for garnish

Place the rice and barley in a medium saucepan. Add water to cover by 1" (2.5 cm). Bring to a boil. Turn down the heat. Cover and simmer until tender, about 10–15 minutes, depending on the type of rice used. Drain off excess water.

Place in a serving bowl. Add the raisins, nuts and parsley. Toss with a few spoonfuls of Vinaigrette or your favourite dressing. Serve at room temperature on a lettuce leaf—and pass the dressing!

DOUBLE MELON SALAD

This salad makes a refreshing early brunch. Serve with Vegetable Omelette or Prawn Frittata with Sun-Dried Tomatoes.

1	cantaloupe, peeled
	sherry
2 cups (500 mL)	honeydew melon balls
	springs of mint for garnish
	Fruit Dressing, page 48

Slice the cantaloupe into rings about 1" (2.5 cm) thick. Remove seeds. Place on a plate and sprinkle with a little sherry. Place the melon balls into a bowl and sprinkle with a little sherry. Chill the cantaloupe and melon balls well.

When ready to serve, place the cantaloupe ring on a small plate. Fill the centre with the balls. Garnish with mint and serve with Fruit Dressing.

PAPAYA AND PEPPER SALAD

Make this salad ahead of time and serve while the lasagne or chicken is cooking.

1/2	papaya, peeled and seeded
1/2	medium red bell pepper, seeded
2	green onions
1/2	English cucumber, peeled and seeded
	Egg Vinaigrette, page 45
	salad greens

Dice the papaya, pepper, onion and cucumber into small pieces. Place in a medium bowl. Make the vinaigrette. Toss some of it with the vegetables. Place the salad greens on chilled salad plates. Spoon on the diced mixture. Drizzle on a little more dressing or pass it at the table.

MELON-TOMATO SALAD

Prepare this salad well ahead of time and chill for a refreshing treat on a hot day. It keeps well in the refrigerator.

1/2	English cucumber, cut into chunks, (peeled and seeded, if desired)
1	small honeydew melon, peeled, seeded and cut into chunks
1/2 lb. (250 g)	thin-skinned tomatoes, seeded, drained and roughly cut
1/2 cup (125 mL)	Vinaigrette, page 44
	butter lettuce leaves
	Toasted Cashews, recipe follows
	mint sprig

Taste the cucumber. If it seems watery or a little bitter, place the chunks on a large platter and sprinkle with salt. Let stand about 1/2 hour. Rinse off the salt and pat dry.

Place the melon, tomatoes and cucumber in an attractive serving bowl. Add the Vinaigrette and mix well. Cover and chill for at least 1 hour. Stir before serving.

To serve, place a leaf of butter lettuce on a chilled salad plate and spoon on the melon mixture. Sprinkle with toasted cashews. Garnish with a sprig of mint and serve with hot bread.

Toasted Cashews

To toast the cashews, place on a baking sheet. Bake at 350° F (180° C) for approximately 8–10 minutes, or until golden and toasted. Watch carefully, as nuts burn easily.

VINAIGRETTE

This is a basic dressing that is useful to have on hand. It multiplies and stores well. **Makes 1 cup (250 mL).**

3/4 cup (175 mL)	mixed vegetable and olive oils
4 tbsp. (60 mL)	white wine vinegar
1	clove garlic, chopped
pinch	dry mustard
1/4 tsp. (1 mL)	mixed fresh herbs, optional, such as chives, mint, parsley, thyme
	salt and pepper to taste

Blend all ingredients well.

SWEET AND SOUR VINAIGRETTE

Makes 2 cups (500 mL).

1 cup (250 mL)	light vegetable oil
3/4 cup (175 mL)	white vinegar
1/2 cup (125 mL)	sugar
2 tbsp. (30 mL)	soy sauce
1/2 tsp. (2 mL)	dry mustard
1/4 tsp. (1 mL)	freshly ground black pepper

Blend all the ingredients well.

EGG VINAIGRETTE

This rich mixture suits a firm salad. **Makes 3/4 cup (175 mL).**

1	hard-cooked egg
1 tsp. (5 mL)	Dijon mustard
1	clove garlic, mashed
2 tbsp. (30 mL)	wine vinegar
8 tbsp. (120 mL)	olive oil
2 tbsp. (30 mL)	chopped parsley, dill *or* tarragon
1 tbsp. (15 mL)	capers
1/4 tsp. (1 mL)	salt
	freshly ground pepper

Peel the egg and cut it in half. Remove the yolk and mash it with the mustard and garlic. Stir in the vinegar. Slowly drizzle in the oil, whisking constantly, until thickened. Add the herbs and capers.

Dice the white of the egg and add it to the sauce. Season to taste.

BALSAMIC VINAIGRETTE

Balsamic vinegar is a mellow dark vinegar that has been aged in oak barrels for many years. Sherry wine vinegar can be substituted, but it doesn't have the same effect. **Makes 1 1/3 cup (325 mL).**

1/3 cup (75 mL)	balsamic vinegar
1 tsp. (5 mL)	lemon juice
pinch	dry mustard
1	small shallot, minced
	finely chopped thyme to taste
	salt and pepper to taste
1 cup (250 mL)	olive oil

In a small bowl, mix together the vinegar, juice, mustard, shallot and seasonings. Slowly whisk in the olive oil to make a creamy vinaigrette.

FRENCH DRESSING

Makes 1 1/2 cup (375 mL).

3/4 cup (175 mL)	oil
1/3 cup (75 mL)	vinegar
1/4 - 1/2 cup (60 - 125 mL)	chili sauce, or to taste
2 - 3 tbsp. (30 - 45 mL)	sugar, or to taste
1 tsp. (5 mL)	Dijon mustard
1 tsp. (5 mL)	dried oregano
1 tsp. (5 mL)	salt
1/4 tsp. (1 mL)	pepper
1/2 tsp. (2 mL)	paprika

Combine all ingredients in a blender or jar with a lid. Cover and mix well. Serve over a mixed green salad.

GREEN GODDESS DRESSING

Makes 1 1/2 cups (375 mL).

4 tbsp. (60 mL)	finely chopped green bell pepper
4 tbsp. (60 mL)	green onions, chopped
4 tbsp. (60 mL)	chopped parsley
1 tbsp. (15 mL)	finely chopped anchovies (3 strips)
1	clove garlic, finely chopped
1/4	bunch watercress, finely chopped
1 cup (250 mL)	mayonnaise

Combine all ingredients in the blender in the order given. Blend well. Serve over mixed greens.

OIL AND VINEGAR DRESSING

Substitute oregano for the basil in the Basil Oil and Vinegar, if desired. Or make the basic oil and vinegar without any special herb and steep a stalk of a fresh herb in the jar. Its flavour will enhance the vinaigrette. **Makes 1 cup (250 mL).**

1/2 cup (125 mL)	olive oil
5 tbsp. (75 mL)	red wine vinegar
1	clove garlic, crushed
1 tsp. (5 mL)	dried oregano
1/2 tsp. (2 mL)	salt
1/4 tsp. (1 mL)	freshly ground pepper

Combine in a jar with a lid. Cover and shake well. Serve over green salad.

Variations

DILLED OIL AND VINEGAR

To the basic dressing, add 4 tbsp. (60 mL) chopped fresh dill or 1 tbsp. (5 mL) dried dill.

BASIL OIL AND VINEGAR

To the basic dressing, add 4 tbsp. (60 mL) chopped fresh basil or 1 tbsp. (5 mL) dried basil.

TARRAGON OIL AND VINEGAR

To the basic dressing, add 4 tbsp. (60 mL) chopped fresh tarragon. Do not use dried tarragon as it does not have a strong enough flavour.

SPICY DRESSING

Makes 1 cup (250 mL).

2/3 cup (150 mL)	light oil
1/3 cup (75 mL)	fresh lemon juice *or* vinegar *or* a mixture of both
1	clove garlic, chopped
1	egg
2 tbsp. (30 mL)	Worcestershire sauce
2 tbsp. (30 mL)	anchovy paste
2 tbsp. (30 mL)	Dijon mustard
2 tbsp. (30 mL)	Parmesan cheese
	seasoned salt
	freshly ground pepper

Put all ingredients into a jar and shake very well. Taste. If the mixture is too oily, add more lemon juice or vinegar. If it is too acidy, add more oil.

FRUIT DRESSING

This slightly sweet and sour dressing complements most fruits.

1	egg
2 tbsp. (30 mL)	sugar
4 tbsp. (60 mL)	dry sherry
4 tbsp. (60 mL)	orange juice
2 tbsp. (30 mL)	lemon juice
2 tsp. (10 mL)	butter
pinch	salt
4 tbsp. (60 mL)	whipping cream

In a medium saucepan, beat together the egg and the sugar. Add the remaining ingredients, except the whipping cream. Cook, stirring constantly, until slightly thickened. Cool and chill. At serving time, whip the cream until slightly thickened and fold into the mixture.

HOMEMADE MAYONNAISE

This mayonnaise will keep up to ten days in the refrigerator. **Makes 1 1/2 cups (375 mL).**

1	egg
1 tsp. (5 mL)	Dijon mustard
1 tsp. (5 mL)	fresh lemon juice
1 tsp. (5 mL)	red *or* white wine vinegar
1 1/2 cups (375 mL)	oil, a mixture of 3 tbsp. (45 mL) olive oil and the rest vegetable oil
	salt and pepper, optional

In a blender or food processor, whirl together the egg, mustard, lemon juice and vinegar. With the machine running, very slowly pour in the oil until the mixture becomes thick and shiny.

The mayonnaise should not need seasoning, but a tiny pinch of salt and/ or pepper can be added, if desired. Chill.

To make this mayonnaise by hand, place the egg, mustard, lemon juice and vinegar in a small bowl. Mix well. Whisk briskly and very, very slowly, drip in the mixed oils.

Variations

MUSTARD MAYONNAISE

1/2 cup (125 mL)	Homemade Mayonnaise
2 tbsp. (30 mL)	grainy mustard

THE SPOT'S MAYO

1/2 cup (125 mL)	Homemade Mayonnaise
4 tbsp. (60 mL)	chili sauce
1 tbsp. (15 mL)	finely chopped pickle

CHUTNEY MAYONNAISE

1/2 cup (125 mL)	Homemade Mayonnaise
2 tbsp. (30 mL)	chutney

BREADS

The wonderful aroma of freshly baked bread can be enjoyed with the simple recipes for baguette or dilled bread. Both recipes are basic. If you wish, add a few tablespoons of bran, oatmeal, graham flour or rye flour before you add the white flour. For a change of taste, omit the dill or substitute another herb or spice. Raisins, currants or chopped apple make the loaf moist and sweet. And, for a heady perfume in each bite, add chopped orange or lemon peel.

BAGUETTE

This bread is wonderful for sopping up the juices of a spicy stew or soup, or served with a crisp chilled salad. Freeze one loaf and eat the other while it's fresh and warm. This recipe doubles well, but you will need a large food processor to handle the dough.

1 tbsp. (15 mL)	sugar
1 1/4 cup (300 mL)	warm water
1 tbsp. (15 mL)	dry yeast
2 1/2 - 3 cups (625 - 750 mL)	white all purpose flour
1 tsp. (5 mL)	salt

In a small bowl or measuring cup, dissolve the sugar in the warm water. Add the yeast. Let stand 5 minutes, or until bubbling. Stir.

Measure 2 cups (500 mL) of the flour into the food processor bowl. Blend in the salt. When the yeast is ready, with the food processor running, slowly pour into the flour. Add flour as needed until dough forms a ball and pulls away from the sides of the bowl.

Remove the dough from the food processor. On a lightly floured surface, knead dough for a few turns. The dough should be smooth and silky.

Grease a medium bowl. Place dough in it and allow to rise until double, about 1 hour. (If time is short, this rise can be omitted.) Punch down and divide into 2 parts. Shape into long loaves. Place in well-greased baguette pans or on a cookie sheet. Slash on an angle. Brush with egg white for a chewy crust. Let stand for 20–30 minutes.

Bake for 15 minutes at 425° F (220° C), then 20 minutes longer at 350° F (180° C), or until golden and the bottoms sound hollow when tapped. Remove from pans and cool. Wrap in foil to freeze. When ready to serve, reheat in foil.

Opposite: Steamed Clams.

DILLED BREAD

This savoury bread is good with salmon or sole. If you don't think you will eat this loaf of bread within a couple of days, make two small loaves and freeze one.

1 tbsp. (15 mL)	dry yeast
1 tbsp. (15 mL)	sugar
4 tbsp. (60 mL)	warm water
1	small onion, chopped
2 1/2 - 3 cups (625 - 750 mL)	white all purpose flour
2 tsp. (10 mL)	dried dill
1 tsp. (5 mL)	salt
1 cup (250 mL)	creamed cottage cheese, at room temperature
	cornmeal

Combine the yeast, sugar and warm water in a small bowl. Let stand 5 minutes or until bubbling. Stir.

In the food processor, mince the onion using the steel blade by dropping it through the feed tube. Remove the lid. Add 2 cups of the flour, the dill and salt. Replace the lid. With the processor running, add the yeast mixture and cottage cheese. Add the flour as needed until dough forms a ball and pulls away from the sides of the bowl.

Remove the dough from the processor. On a lightly floured surface, knead dough for a few turns. The dough should be smooth and silky.

Grease a medium bowl. Place dough in it and allow to rise until double, about 1 hour. Grease a 1 1/2 qt. (1.5 L) round casserole or soufflé dish (or two small loaf pans) with 3" (7.5 cm) sides. Sprinkle bottom with cornmeal.

Punch the dough down. On a lightly floured surface, shape it into a round loaf. Place in greased dish. Let stand until the dough has risen to about even with the top of the pan, about 30–45 minutes. Brush with egg wash and sprinkle on some coarse salt.

Bake at 350° F (180° C) for 45 minutes, or until loaf sounds hollow when tapped on the bottom. Cool on a rack.

GARLIC BREAD

Baguette or French are the best kinds of bread to use for this garlic bread recipe. But be careful—it's addictive!

1/2 lb. (250 g)	butter
3	cloves garlic, chopped
4 tbsp. (60 mL)	Parmesan cheese
2 tbsp. (30 mL)	chopped fresh parsley
1	loaf sliced French bread

Melt butter. Sauté garlic briefly. Mix together cheese and parsley. Dip only one side of the bread slices in the butter and garlic mixture, then into the cheese and parsley mixture. Stack bread slices in foil.

Bake for 20 minutes at 200° F (100° C). Remove from foil and spread apart on a baking sheet. Cook under the broiler until lightly browned.

MAIN DISHES

Chicken, turkey, beef, lamb, pork, veal, salmon, swordfish, shark, sole, clams, snapper and trout... the list of main dishes goes on! You'll find a variety of interesting main dishes to build a wonderful meal around for the two of you. Try Fricadelles with Tomato Sauce, Dilled Bread and a bowl of Seasonal Fruit, for a casual meal. Or, for more elegant fare, try Grilled Swordfish with Basil Butter, an Antipasto Platter and a Parfait of crème de menthe blended with ice cream.

SIMMERED CHICKEN

A creamy salad dressing, such as Miracle Whip, and soy sauce provide the interesting mixture in which the chicken is simmered. Serve over thin egg noodles. Oranges Jubilee make a fancy dessert.

4	pieces of frying chicken, such as thighs, legs or breasts (2 per person)
2 tbsp. (30 mL)	oil
4	small boiling onions
1- 10 oz. (284 mL) can	chicken broth
1	stalk celery, sliced
3 - 4 tbsp. (45 - 60 mL)	sliced stuffed olives
1/2 cup (125 mL)	salad dressing
1 tbsp. (15 mL)	soy sauce
1 tsp. (5 mL)	cornstach

In a medium skillet, brown the chicken in the oil. Add the onions and chicken broth. Cover and simmer 20 minutes.

Add celery and olives. Combine the salad dressing and soy sauce. Pour over chicken mixture. Simmer for 15 minutes. With a slotted spoon, remove chicken and vegetables to a warm serving platter.

Spoon 2 tbsp. (30 mL) of the liquid into a small dish. Mix in the cornstarch. Bring liquid in the skillet to a boil. Cook, stirring occassionally, for 2–3 minutes. Stir in cornstarch mixture until slightly thickened. Pour over chicken or serve alongside.

CHICKEN BREASTS WITH CURRY MAYONNAISE

For this dish, creamy Curry Mayonnaise is spooned over each chicken breast. Serve with Ranch Cut Potatoes and Hot Spinach Salad.

1	whole chicken breast, halved
1	small carrot, sliced
1	small onion, sliced
2	stalks celery, sliced
	fresh parsley
1	bay leaf
1/2 tsp. (2 mL)	dried thyme
pinch	salt
	fresh ground pepper
1/2 cup (125 mL)	dry white wine
1 1/2 cups (375 mL)	chicken stock
	Curry Mayonnaise, recipe follows

Skin and bone chicken breast. Set aside skin, bones and chicken. Combine remaining ingredients in a large pot and bring to a boil. Add the skin and bones from the chicken and cook 30 minutes. Add the chicken breasts to the liquid and arrange so they are spread flat. Simmer gently for 20 minutes. Do not overcook as the chicken will become dry. Remove from the stock and cool thoroughly.

Arrange chicken breasts on a serving platter. Nap each breast with Curry Mayonnaise.

Curry Mayonnaise

3 tbsp. (45 mL)	Homemade Mayonnaise, page 49
1 tbsp. (15 mL)	Curry Sauce, page 61, or to taste

Mix ingredients and use as directed above.

CHICKEN CURRY

Serve this curry on a bed of basmati rice with small bowls of toasted coconut, raisins and salted nuts as individual garnishes. A cooling dessert of Fruit Compote will hit the spot.

1 tbsp. (15 mL)	butter
1 tbsp. (15 mL)	oil
1	whole chicken breast, halved and cut into 1" (2.5 cm) cubes
1/2 recipe	Curry Sauce, page 61
	several slices of red and green pepper *or* 2 oz. (60 g) seedless red and green grapes and 1/2 small pineapple, peeled, cored and cut into 1" (2.5 cm) cubes

Melt the butter in the oil. Sauté the chicken pieces on all sides, about 2–3 minutes. Add the curry sauce and bring to a boil. Reduce the heat and simmer gently for 5 minutes, or until the chicken is cooked through. Add the peppers or the grapes and pineapple cubes. Simmer another minute.

CURRY SAUCE

Vary this basic recipe according to your taste. The powdered spices can be used in any recipe calling for curry powder. This curry sauce will keep, refrigerated, for several weeks.

2 tbsp. (30 mL)	butter
3	cloves garlic, finely chopped
1	medium onion, finely chopped
1 tbsp. (15 mL)	finely chopped fresh ginger
1/2- 5 1/2 oz. (156 mL) can	tomato paste
1 recipe	Curry Powder, recipe follows
1 1/2 cups (375 mL)	water, chicken stock *or* canned broth
	juice of 3 lemons
	salt and pepper

Melt the butter in a medium saucepan. Gently sauté the garlic, onion and ginger for 1 minute. Add the tomato paste and cook for 1 minute. Add the curry powder. Cook, mixing thoroughly, for 30 seconds to 1 minute until the spices start to release their aroma.

Gradually add the cold water, stock or broth. Bring to a boil. Reduce heat. Simmer, covered, for 1 1/2 hours. Add the lemon juice. Taste and adjust for salt and pepper if desired. Store in a glass jar in the refrigerator.

Curry Powder

Homemade curry powder tastes much better than store bought. A coffee mill used only to grind spices is a great help.

1 tsp. (5 mL)	black pepper corns
1 tsp. (5 mL)	whole mustard seeds
1/2 tsp. (2 mL)	whole coriander seeds
1/2 tsp. (2 mL)	whole cumin seeds
1/2 tsp. (2 mL)	whole fennel seeds
1/2 tsp. (2 mL)	cayenne pepper flakes, optional
1	large bay leaf, broken
8	whole cloves
6 - 12	cardamom seeds (tiny black ones)

In a spice mill or blender, grind all the ingredients together until fine.

If not using right away, store powder in an airtight container in the refrigerator. The powder will keep several weeks.

NOUVELLE CUISINE CHICKEN WITH VEGETABLES

This is a colourful main dish of chicken and vegetables. Start with Nut and Curry Soup as a smooth beginning to the meal.

6	uncooked shelled shrimp
1	whole chicken breast, halved, skinned, boned and cut into strips
2 tbsp. (30 mL)	dry sherry
2 tsp. (10 mL)	soy sauce
1/2 tsp. (2 mL)	chopped fresh ginger
1	clove garlic, minced or chopped
1 - 2 tbsp. (15 - 30 mL)	oil
2 cups (500 mL)	vegetables of your choice, cut into small pieces, including broccoli, red and green peppers, mushrooms, onions, celery, snow peas, cherry tomatoes
4 tbsp. (60 mL)	chicken stock
1 tbsp. (15 mL)	Worcestershire sauce
	salt and pepper

Marinate the shrimp and chicken in the sherry, soy sauce, ginger and garlic for 30 minutes.

Heat oil in a large skillet or wok. Add shrimp and chicken. Stir-fry over medium heat for 3–4 minutes. Remove and set aside on a warm platter.

Add the vegetables, except the tomatoes. Sauté for 4–5 minutes. Add the chicken stock and Worcestershire sauce. Season to taste with salt and pepper. Let boil briefly. Add the chicken and tomatoes. Heat through.

CHICKEN IN PHYLLO

Phyllo (filo) pastry is available frozen in most markets. The best, of course, is the fresh pastry from the Greek bakeries. Carrots Vichy add a vibrant touch of colour to the plate.

1	whole chicken breast, halved, skinned and boned
1 tsp. (5 mL)	butter
1 tsp. (5 mL)	olive oil
1 tbsp. (15 mL)	minced shallot
1	clove garlic, minced
3 - 4	whole fresh mushrooms, sliced
1 tbsp. (15 mL)	chopped parsley
1 tsp. (5 mL)	chopped fresh tarragon
	phyllo pastry
	unsalted butter, melted

Cut each half chicken breast into half again. Lightly sauté the chicken in a mixture of butter and olive oil. Set aside.

In the same skillet, sauté the shallot and garlic. Add the mushrooms. Sauté briefly. Add the herbs and season to taste.

For each piece of chicken, you need 1 sheet of phyllo. Brush each sheet with butter and fold in half. Brush with butter again and place the chicken breast in the centre. Pile a little of the mushroom duxelles on top of the chicken.

Fold the phyllo in on each side, then fold down from the top and up from the bottom to form a package. Place on a baking sheet lined with parchment or foil. Brush all with butter. The dish may be made ahead to this point and frozen or refrigerated.

An hour before serving time, remove chicken packages from the refrigerator. Let sit at room temperature. Brush with melted butter mixed with a little parsley. Bake at 375° F (190° C) for 20–25 minutes, or until puffed and golden.

COCONUT CHICKEN

This is Sunday chicken with a twist—coconut, raisins, apple and curry are added! Serve any leftovers for a light lunch the next day. Try this dish with Spaghetti Squash.

3 tbsp. (45 mL)	oil
1	small onion, chopped
1 - 1 1/2 lb. (500 - 750 g)	chicken legs and thighs
4 tbsp. (60 mL)	raisins
4 tbsp. (60 mL)	flaked unsweetened coconut
1	medium apple, unpeeled and diced
1- 10 oz. (284 mL) can	cream of mushroom soup
pinch	curry powder, or to taste
	chopped salted peanuts, optional

Heat 1 tbsp. (15 mL) of the oil in a large skillet. Add the onion and sauté until tender. Place in a 1 1/2 qt. (1.5 L) casserole.

Add remaining oil to the skillet. Add the chicken and brown on all sides. Put chicken in casserole as it browns. Add the raisins, coconut and apple.

Add soup and curry powder to drippings in skillet. Bring to a boil, scraping up brown bits. Pour over chicken.

Cover and bake at 425° F (220° C) for 45 minutes, or until chicken is tender. Top with chopped nuts.

FRUIT-STUFFED CHICKEN

In this dish, nuts, raisins and apricots are stuffed under the skin of a boned chicken breast and baked. Serve with Cream Sauce and Celery Root Julienne.

4 tbsp. (60 mL)	sultana raisins
4 tbsp. (60 mL)	chopped dried apricots
4 tbsp. (60 mL)	chopped nuts, such as pine nuts, pecans *or* walnuts
1	whole chicken breast, halved, boned but NOT skinned
1	egg, beaten
4 tbsp. (60 mL)	fine dry bread crumbs
1 tsp. (5 mL)	paprika
4 tbsp. (60 mL)	melted butter
	Cream Sauce, recipe follows

Mix together the raisins, apricots and nuts. Push the mixture under the chicken skin, spreading evenly over the meat. Pull the skin smooth. The dish may be made ahead to this point.

Place the egg in a small flat dish. In another dish, mix the bread crumbs with the paprika. Dip the stuffed chicken into the egg, then into the bread crumbs. Place chicken on a small baking sheet.

Bake at 375° F (190° C) for 30 minutes. Baste with the butter halfway through the cooking time. When done, spoon Cream Sauce over chicken and serve.

Cream Sauce

This creamed reduction sauce is very quick to make and can be served with many baked or sautéed meats.

2 tbsp. (30 mL)	finely chopped onion
2 tbsp. (30 mL)	butter
1 cup (250 mL)	dry white wine *or* chicken broth
1 cup (250 mL)	whipping cream
pinch	chopped fresh tarragon *or* parsley
	salt and pepper to taste

In a small saucepan, sauté the onion in the butter. Add the wine and bring to a boil. Boil until the wine is reduced by half. Add the cream and bring to a boil. Reduce heat to medium low. Cook to reduce mixture by half. The sauce will be thick and creamy. Stir in the herbs. Taste and adjust for seasonings.

CHICKEN VERONIQUE CRÊPES

Make a batch of crêpes on a rainy Sunday and freeze in packages of four or eight. Two filled crêpes make a satisfying meal for most people when served with a salad or soup. Serve this dish with Sauté of Green Beans.

1 1/2 cups (375 mL)	cubed cooked chicken
1/2 cup (125 mL)	seedless green grapes, halved
5 tbsp. (75 mL)	toasted slivered almonds
4 tbsp. (60 mL)	chopped celery
2 tbsp. (30 mL)	chopped green onion
1/2 tsp. (2 mL)	freshly ground pepper
1/2 cup (125 mL)	mayonnaise
1/2 cup (125 mL)	sour cream
2 tbsp. (30 mL)	dry white wine
1 tsp. (5 mL)	Dijon mustard
4	7" (18 cm) crêpes
	fresh mint sprigs and grapes for garnish

In a large bowl, combine chicken, grapes, 4 tbsp. (60 mL) of the toasted slivered almonds, celery, onion and pepper. Mix gently.

In a small bowl, combine mayonnaise, sour cream, white wine and mustard. Mix well. Set aside 1/2 the mayonnaise mixture. Fold the remaining mayonnaise mixture into chicken mixture. Spoon about 1/2 cup (125 mL) chicken filling onto each crêpe. Roll up. Place seam side down in a greased baking dish. Cover.

Bake at 375° F (190° C) for 20–25 minutes, or until heated through. Top with a dollop of the reserved mayonnaise mixture and the remaining toasted almonds. Garnish with mint and grapes.

CRISPY CHICKEN ROLLS

These chicken breasts are stuffed with chopped shrimp and onion, then deep-fried. They can be sliced and served at room temperature as an appetizer. Or place them on top of shredded lettuce or Warm Red Cabbage for a light lunch.

1/4 lb. (125 g)	cooked shelled shrimp
2	whole large chicken breasts, skinned, boned and halved
6 tbsp. (120 mL)	soft butter
2 tbsp. (30 mL)	chopped green onion
	freshly ground pepper to taste
	oil
1/2 cup (125 mL)	white all purpose flour
3/4 tsp. (3 mL)	baking powder
1/2 cup (125 mL)	water

Chop shrimp and set aside. Pound chicken breasts to about 1/4" (5 mm) thickness.

In a medium bowl, combine shrimp, butter, green onions and pepper. Spoon mixture onto centres of breasts, leaving 1/2" (1 cm) edge around each. From narrow end, roll each breast jelly-roll fashion and fasten with toothpicks. Cover and refrigerate rolls at least 15 minutes to firm.

Meanwhile, in a deep skillet or saucepan, heat 1" (2.5 cm) of oil to 375° F (190° C).

In a medium bowl, mix flour, reserving 1 tbsp. (15 mL), with baking powder and water until well blended. Dust the chicken rolls with the reserved 1 tbsp. (15 mL) of the flour, then roll in batter to coat all sides.

Lower into hot oil in skillet. Fry until golden, 10–15 minutes, turning occasionally. Drain chicken rolls on paper towels. Remove and discard toothpicks. Keep warm if eating right away. Cool and refrigerate if using later.

Reheat the chicken on HIGH for 2–3 minutes in the microwave, if desired.

SWEET AND SOUR TURKEY WINGS

Choose the turkey wings according to your appetite—they can be quite large.
Serve this dish over rice, noodles or mashed potatoes with Minted Snow Peas.

2	turkey wings
1 - 2 tbsp. (15 - 30 mL)	oil
1/2 - 3/4 cup (125 - 175 mL)	chicken broth *or* water
1 tbsp. (15 mL)	cornstarch
2 tbsp. (30 mL)	packed brown sugar
2 tbsp. (30 mL)	each, vinegar and soy sauce
2 tbsp. (30 mL)	chili sauce

Disjoint wings. Set tip aside for another use. Brown wings in the oil in a medium skillet. Add 1/2 cup (125 mL) of the broth. Reduce heat. Cover and cook for 1 1/2–2 hours, or until tender.

Remove wings from skillet. Measure out liquid. Add enough broth or water to make 3/4 cup (175 mL). Whisk in the cornstarch. Pour back into skillet. Add the remaining ingredients. Cook, stirring, until smooth and thickened. Return wings to the pan and heat through.

CHOPPED TURKEY ON TOAST

Cooked turkey is usually available in the deli section of most markets. This dish is wonderful with Cream of Potato Soup (hot Vichyssoise).

1 cup (250 mL)	chopped cooked turkey *or* chicken
1	small apple, peeled and chopped
1	stalk celery, chopped
1 - 2 tbsp. (15 - 30 mL)	finely chopped green onion
1 tbsp. (15 mL)	chopped parsley
3 - 4 tbsp. (45 - 60 mL)	mayonnaise
pinch	curry powder to taste
	freshly ground pepper to taste
2	slices white bread, toasted and buttered
	paprika

In a medium bowl, mix together the turkey, apple, celery, onion and parsley.

In a small bowl, mix together the mayonnaise, curry powder and pepper. Stir into turkey mixture.

Arrange the toast on a baking sheet, buttered side up. Divide turkey mixture between them. Broil 4–6" (10–15 cm) from heat for 4–5 minutes, or until heated through. Sprinkle with paprika.

PERFECT GRILLED STEAK

For this recipe, ask your butcher to cut a 1 1/2" (3 cm) striploin or tenderloin steak for you. Serve with Ranch Cut Potatoes or Potato Hash with Red and Green Peppers and Chocolate Valentine's Cake for dessert—with a scoop of French vanilla ice cream!

	crushed black peppercorns, optional
1	small steak, per person
1/2 cup (125 mL)	chicken stock *or* canned broth
1/2 cup (125 mL)	whipping cream

Heat the grill or a medium skillet to medium-hot. Press the peppercorns into the steak, if desired. Grill or sauté the meat about 5 minutes on each side for medium-rare. Remove from the pan.

Add the chicken stock to the skillet and bring to a boil. Boil until reduced by half. Add the whipping cream and bring to a boil. Reduce heat and simmer until thickened. Spoon over steak and serve.

Opposite: Nouvelle Cuisine Chicken with Vegetables.

EASY HOMEMADE SPANISH RICE

Cook this rice dish up in bulk, freeze in 1 cup (250 mL) portions and you have a main dish ready for numerous dinners. Serve with Baked Onions for a hearty meal.

1/2 lb. (250 g)	lean ground beef
4 tbsp. (60 mL)	each, chopped onion and green bell pepper
pinch	salt
1 cup (250 mL)	cooked rice
1/2 cup (125 mL)	shredded cheddar cheese
1- 7.5 oz. (213 mL) can	tomato sauce

Brown the ground beef with the onion and green pepper. Pour off the fat. Add the salt. Stir in the rice and cheese. Pour in the tomato sauce. Heat through or microwave on MEDIUM (50%) or MEDIUM HIGH (80%) for 5 minutes, or until heated through.

FRICADELLES WITH TOMATO AND MUSHROOM SAUCE

Fricadelles are little beef and pork meatballs that you grind yourself in the food processor. Handle the mixture lightly to keep the meat tender. Serve with Dilled Bread and Seasonal Fruit with Rosewater.

1/2 lb. (250 g)	beef steak, cut into 1" (2.5 cm) chunks
1/4 lb. (125 g)	pork tenderloin, cut into 1" (2.5 cm) chunks
2	shallots *or* 1/2 small onion
	fresh herbs to taste, such as parsley, chives, savoury
1	slice of bread, crusts removed, soaked in milk
1	egg
	salt and pepper
	flour
2 tbsp. (30 mL)	butter
1 tbsp. (15 mL)	olive oil
	Tomato and Mushroom Sauce, recipe follows

In the food processor, chop the meat in small batches. Place in mixing bowl. Chop the shallots and herbs in the processor. Add bread and mix. Add mixture to meat in bowl. Add egg. Season well with salt and pepper to taste. Form into balls.

Roll in flour. Flatten and brown in hot butter and olive oil. Transfer to an ovenproof dish and bake at 375° F (190° C) for 5 minutes. Serve with fresh Tomato and Mushroom Sauce.

Tomato and Mushroom Sauce

1/4 lb. (125 g)	fresh mushrooms, cleaned
	butter
4 - 5	medium tomatoes, seeded
	fresh herbs, such as parsley, chives, savoury, thyme
	salt and pepper to taste
	sugar to taste
	whipping cream, optional

In a food processor with the slicing blade, slice the mushrooms. Transfer to a skillet and brown in butter. Process the tomatoes with the fresh herbs. Add tomato mixture to mushrooms and simmer until thickened slightly. Season to taste with salt, pepper and sugar. Add up to 1/2 cup (125 mL) of whipping cream, if desired.

MEXICANA BUNWICHES

These bunwiches are good on the menu for a late Sunday lunch. They are quick and easy to make.

1/2 lb. (250 g)	lean ground beef
4 tbsp. (60 mL)	chopped onion
4 tbsp. (60 mL)	chopped green bell pepper
1/4 lb. (125 g)	frankfurters, sliced
pinch	pure chili powder, or to taste
pinch	dried oregano
pinch	freshly ground pepper
1/2 cup (125 mL)	tomato sauce
2	hamburger buns, split and toasted

In a skillet, sauté the beef with the onion and green pepper until onion is tender. Pour off fat. Add frankfurters, chili powder, oregano and pepper. Pour on tomato sauce. Simmer 5 minutes. Spoon over buns and serve.

RACK OF LAMB FOR TWO

Rack of lamb is delightful for an intimate dinner for two. Make sure the butcher has taken out the chine bone and trimmed the tips. This will already be done for you in the small frozen racks. Serve the lamb with Cream of Broccoli Soup and Potato Hash with Red and Green Peppers. Strawberry Meringues are a must for dessert!

2   small racks of lamb
olive oil
dried *or* fresh herbs, such as rosemary, thyme, sage, oregano
cloves of garlic, slivered

Place the racks on a baking sheet with the tips interlocking. Rub with olive oil. Generously sprinkle on the herbs. With the tip of a knife, make a few incisions in the meat. Insert the slivered garlic.

Place in a 450° F (230° C) oven and roast for 30 minutes. Let stand for 5 minutes before serving. The meat will be pink and moist.

GRILLED KEBABS OF LAMB WITH CUMIN AND GINGER

Wonderful Middle Eastern aromas are created by this dish, which cooks in about 7 minutes. It serves two people for two days. Serve with a Carrot Salad in Lettuce Cups on the first day. Sliver the leftovers and mix instead of the chicken in Chunky Chicken Salad on the second day.

1	small lamb roast, boned
4 tbsp. (60 mL)	oil
2 tbsp. (30 mL)	fresh ginger, peeled and finely chopped
1 - 2	cloves garlic, crushed
2 tsp. (10 mL)	ground cumin
2 tsp. (10 mL)	ground coriander
pinch	each, salt and cayenne

Start the barbecue or broiler.

Trim the lamb and cut into 1 1/2" (3.5 cm) cubes. Set aside. In a small bowl, mix together the remaining ingredients until well blended. Add the lamb and stir well. Let stand.

Thread the lamb on skewers, leaving a small space between each piece. Place on a greased grill about 4" (10 cm) from the heat. Barbecue or grill about 3 minutes on each side, or until done to your liking. Serve immediately.

BROILED LAMB CHOPS WITH STIR-FRIED SPINACH

This quick and delicious dish calls for spring lamb loin chops. Tiny new pota-toes are boiled and tossed in butter and parsley. Serve with a delectable dessert of Old-Fashioned Strawberry Shortcake with Devon-Style Cream.

6	lamb loin chops (3 per person)
1 tsp. (5 mL)	lemon zest
4 tbsp. (60 mL)	fresh lemon juice
	salt and pepper to taste
1 tbsp. (15 mL)	oil
1	clove of garlic, minced
10 oz. (300 g)	fresh spinach, washed and dried
	juice of 1/2 lemon

Trim any fat from the chops. Divide the lemon zest between the chops, pressing well into the meat. Place on a broiler rack and drizzle lemon juice over all. Let stand while the broiler is heating.

When the broiler is hot, place the chops about 4" (10 cm) from the heat. Broil about 4 minutes. Turn and broil on the other side for 3–4 minutes, or until done to your liking (slash into the meat to check). Season with salt and pepper.

While the meat is cooking, heat the oil in a wok or a large frypan, swirl-ing the oil to coat the pan. Add the garlic, spinach and lemon juice. Stir-fry over medium heat until the spinach is just wilted and flavoured, about 2–3 minutes. Season with salt and pepper.

Divide the spinach among the serving plates and place chops on it. Serve immediately.

TOMATO AND CHEESE VEAL CUTLETS

Veal makes a good meal for two because most cuts are sold in small portions. It is a tender meat and cooks quickly. Serve these cutlets with Fresh Corn Soup and Fruit Compote.

2- 3 - 4 oz. (90 - 125 g)	veal cutlets
1 tbsp. (15 mL)	oil
1	clove garlic, minced
1- 7.5 oz. (213 mL)	tomato sauce
1 tbsp. (15 mL)	chopped parsley
1 tsp. (5 mL)	Worcestershire sauce
1/2 tsp. (2 mL)	dried oregano
3 tbsp. (45 mL)	grated cheddar cheese

In a large skillet, brown the cutlets in the oil. Sauté the garlic for 1 or 2 minutes.

Mix together the tomato sauce, parsley, Wocestershire and oregano. Pour over meat in skillet. Sprinkle on cheese. Cover and simmer for 10–15 minutes, or until cutlets are tender, or microwave on MEDIUM (50%) or MEDIUM HIGH (80%), covered, for 4–5 minutes, or until cheese melts and cutlets are tender.

EASY DEVILLED CHOPS

Serve these tasty chops with Rice Pilaf and a tossed green salad.

4	thin pork chops
4 tbsp. (60 mL)	chopped onion
4 tbsp. (60 mL)	chopped green bell pepper
2 tsp. (10 mL)	Worcestershire sauce
1 tsp. (5 mL)	Dijon mustard
1- 7.5 oz. (213 mL) can	tomato sauce

In a medium skillet with lid, brown the pork chops. Stir in onion, green pepper, Worcestershire sauce and mustard. Pour in tomato sauce. Simmer, covered, turning at half time, for 30 minutes, or microwave on MEDIUM (50%) or MEDIUM HIGH (80%), covered, for 6–7 minutes, or until meat is done.

ORIENTAL PORK

Ginger, bamboo shoots and soy sauce flavour this pork dish, which is quickly stir-fried. Frozen brussels sprouts are the surprise ingredient and provide a bit of green color. Serve over steamed white rice garnished with bright red pimento strips.

1/2 lb. (250 g)	raw pork, cut into 2" (5 cm) strips
1 tbsp. (5 mL)	oil
1- 8 oz. (227 mL) can	water chestnuts, undrained
3/4 cup (175 mL)	chicken broth
1 tbsp. (15 mL)	cornstarch
2 tbsp. (30 mL)	dry sherry
2 tbsp. (30 mL)	soy sauce
1/2 tsp. (2 mL)	chopped fresh gingerroot
dash	freshly ground pepper
1- 10 oz. (300 g) pkg.	frozen brussels sprouts
1- 2 oz. (57 mL) jar	sliced red pimentos
1/2 cup (125 mL)	sliced green onions, tops included
3 or 4	fresh whole mushrooms, sliced

In a large wok or skillet, sauté the pork in oil until browned on all sides, stirring frequently.

In a small bowl, gradually stir liquid from the water chestnuts and the chicken broth into the cornstarch. Stir until smooth. Add sherry, soy sauce, gingerroot and pepper.

Stir liquid mixture into wok with pork. Cook until thickened, about 1 minute, stirring frequently. Add brussels sprouts. Cover and steam according to package directions until almost tender.

Set a few sliced pimentos aside for garnish. Stir remaining pimentos, the green onions, mushrooms and reserved water chestnuts into wok. Cover and cook about 3 minutes until all vegetables are tender.

WILD MUSHROOMS AND BACON SAUTÉ

Prepare all the ingredients ahead of time and toss over medium heat just before serving. This dish—with a poached egg nestled on top—makes a terrific brunch. For variety, try different vegetables, such as slivers of celery root, fennel or endive. **Serves 2 as a main dish or 4 as a side dish**.

6	small to medium carrots
2	stalks celery *or* 3/4 lb. (375 g) of various vegetables
4 oz. (125 g)	shiitake mushrooms
3 tbsp. (45 mL)	butter
2 tbsp. (30 mL)	vegetable oil
1	shallot *or* green onion, finely chopped
1	clove garlic, finely minced
8	slices of bacon
1 tbsp. (15 mL)	lemon juice
	salt and freshly ground pepper
	fresh parsley, chopped

Trim and peel the carrots and celery. Cut into strips about 1/4" (5 mm) long. Cook in boiling salted water until just barely tender, about 5–8 minutes. Drain and reserve.

Remove the mushroom stems and cut the remainder into thick strips. Heat 1 tbsp. (15 mL) each of the butter and oil in a medium skillet. Add the shallot and garlic. Cook gently until tender. Add the remaining butter and oil. Stir in the mushrooms. Toss frequently until lightly browned. Drain and reserve.

Fry the bacon and crumble coarsely. Drain and reserve. The dish may be made ahead to this point.

Just before serving, reheat the skillet. Add the vegetables and toss to heat. Add the mushrooms and bacon. Cook, tossing frequently, until heated through, about 5 minutes. Add the lemon juice and salt and pepper to taste. Sprinkle with parsley. Serve immediately.

GRILLED SALMON

These salmon fillets can be grilled over the barbecue or in the oven. Serve with tiny new potatoes that have been steamed, then tossed in oil or butter with chopped basil and parsley. Spread a flavourful mayonnaise over the fish for a final tasty touch.

2	medium salmon fillets *or* steaks
	butter

Place fillets or steaks side by side on an oiled rack. Place over the hot coals, skin side up, with 1 oz. (30 g) butter on each piece at the thickest part. When the butter starts to melt, brush over the skin. Turn the fish and place another pat of butter on each fillet. As it melts, brush over the fish. The fish will be done by the time the butter is completely melted. It will flake easily. The total cooking time will not be more than 20–30 minutes, depending on the thickness of the fish.

To bake the salmon in an oven, place the fillets on oiled foil on a baking sheet, skin side down. Heat the oven to 450° F (230 °C). Bake, brushing with butter, for 20 minutes, or until meat flakes easily.

Serve from the grill. Lift the meat from the skin. Serve with a flavoured mayonnaise. Some suggestions are below.

Flavoured Mayonnaises

Begin with a great mayonnaise, then add flavourings as described here.

1/2 cup (125 mL)	mayonnaise
2 tbsp. (30 mL)	grainy mustard

or

1/2 cup (125 mL)	mayonnaise
4 tbsp. (60 mL)	chili sauce
1 tbsp. (15 mL)	finely chopped pickle

or

1/2 cup (125 mL)	mayonnaise
2 tbsp. (30 mL)	mango chutney

STIR-FRIED SALMON CHUNKS

Served with a nutty brown rice, this salmon dish makes a tasty meal for one. It can be multiplied for up to four (increase the cooking time accordingly). Substitute thin slivers of beef, if desired. **Serves 1**.

2 tbsp. (30 mL)	oil
1	medium salmon steak, cut into 1" (2.5 cm) cubes
1	green onion, sliced on the diagonal a few slices of red onion
1 tbsp. (15 mL)	soy sauce
3 - 4	snow pea pods, slivered slivers of fresh oyster mushrooms, optional salt and pepper to taste

Heat the oil in a wok or medium skillet on medium heat. Add the salmon cubes and sear on all sides. Add the green and red onion along with the soy sauce. Toss gently. Cover and cook for 2 minutes. Add the pea pods and mushrooms. Cover and cook for 1 minute. Taste for seasoning, adding salt and pepper, if desired. Serve immediately.

SALMON SOUFFLÉ IN TOMATO

Beautiful canned B.C. sockeye is the fish for this quickie. Or use any leftover cooked salmon. Serve on a lettuce leaf with lots of bread and butter. This dish can be baked in individual ramekins or in one soufflé dish.

1- 7.5 oz. (213 g) can	sockeye salmon
1	egg, separated
1	egg white
4 tbsp. (60 mL)	mayonnaise
4 tbsp. (60 mL)	chopped celery
2 tbsp. (30 mL)	pickle relish
1 tbsp. (15 mL)	Dijon mustard
1 tsp. (5 mL)	lemon juice
pinch	cayenne pepper
	salt and pepper to taste
8	medium tomatoes

Preheat oven to 400° F (200° C).

Drain and flake the salmon into a medium bowl. Add the egg yolk. In another bowl, beat the 2 egg whites until stiff. Stir the remaining ingredients, except the tomatoes, into the salmon mixture. Fold in the beaten egg whites.

Slice a small amount of skin off the bottom of the tomatoes so that they will stand up perfectly straight. Slice off the topcaps and scoop out the pulp. Turn tomatoes upside down to drain.

Spoon the salmon mixture into the tomato cups. Do not overfill. Bake until puffed and golden, about 20 minutes. (A large soufflé dish will bake in 1 hour.)

FILLET OF RED SNAPPER

Serve Cocktail de la Mer du Nord as a crisp first course to this delectable dish of snapper and creamy mashed potatoes.

2	medium red snapper fillets
pinch	each, chopped fresh basil, salt and pepper to taste
	juice of 1/2 lemon
	flour
2 tbsp. (30 mL)	olive oil
4 - 6	fresh mushrooms, sliced
1- 6 1/2 oz. (184 mL) jar	marinated artichoke hearts
1	clove garlic, minced
2	fresh tomatoes, seeded and chopped
1/3 cup (75 mL)	white wine
2 tbsp. (30 mL)	bread crumbs
	Duchess Potatoes, recipe follows

Season snapper fillets with basil, salt, pepper and lemon juice. Dip each side in flour. In a skillet, sauté in hot oil for 2 minutes on each side. Remove to greased baking dish.

In the skillet, sauté the mushrooms, artichokes and garlic. Add tomatoes and cook briefly. Spoon over the fish. Pour on the wine and sprinkle on the bread crumbs. Bake at 375° F (190° C) for 10 minutes, or until fish is almost done.

Remove from oven. Garnish with Duchess Potatoes piped through a pastry tube or spread around the edges. Return to oven and bake until potatoes are lightly browned. The fish should flake easily and the sauce should be heated through.

Duchess Potatoes

2	medium potatoes
2	egg yolks
1 tbsp. (15 mL)	butter
pinch	nutmeg
	salt and pepper to taste

Boil and mash potatoes. Beat in the egg yolks, butter, nutmeg, salt and pepper. Mix lightly.

HALIBUT BROCHETTES

The flavour of this marinade permeates the flesh of the fish within 30 minutes. Use leftover sauce to brush on while grilling or for dipping. Serve Tapenade Dip while waiting for the coals to heat.

1/2 lb. (250 g)	halibut, per person
	small onions
	cherry tomatoes
1/2 cup (125 mL)	soy sauce
4 tbsp. (60 mL)	sherry
1 tbsp. (15 mL)	vegetable oil
1 tbsp. (15 mL)	sugar, optional
1 - 2 tsp. (5 - 10 mL)	minced fresh ginger
1	clove garlic, minced

Cut the fish into 1" (2.5 cm) cubes. Thread fish on skewers, alternating with the onions and tomatoes. Mix together the remaining ingredients. Pour into a flat glass container that will hold the skewers. Marinade the fish for approximately 30 minutes, turning several times.

Broil skewers over hot charcoal or in a preheated broiler. Turn frequently and brush with marinade until the meat is golden brown on all sides, about 10–15 minutes.

SOLE WITH MUSTARD GLAZE

Cooked under the broiler and brushed with a tangy glaze, this sole dish is absolutely delicious. Try it with Spinach with Nuts or Casserole Peas.

2	medium fillets of sole
3 tbsp. (45 mL)	soft butter
2 tbsp. (30 mL)	Dijon or other flavourful mustard
1 tbsp. (15 mL)	fresh lemon juice
dash	paprika
	salt and pepper to taste

Heat the broiler and place the fish on a broiler rack.

Mix together the remaining ingredients to form a soft basting sauce. Add more lemon juice if necessary. Brush one side of the fish. Broil about 3" (7.5 cm) from the heat for about 3–4 minutes, or until the mustard sauce is bubbling. Turn the fish over very carefully because it is fragile. Brush the other side. Broil again until done. Serve with additional sauce.

Opposite: Grilled Salmon.

COD STEAKS WITH BROWN BUTTER

Cod is good for grilling or skewer recipes because it does not break easily. Pumpkin Conserve makes a colourful addition to this dish. Serve with Vegetable Fritters.

1/2 lb. (250 g)	cod steak, per person
	Brown Butter Sauce, recipe follows

Grill over medium-high heat. Set on warmed serving plates. Prepare Brown Butter Sauce.

Brown Butter Sauce

1 tbsp. (15 mL)	butter, per person
	chopped parsley *or* green onions

Place butter in a small skillet. Cook over high heat until butter foams and begins to turn a rich golden brown. Immediately remove from heat and pour over the cooked fish. Scatter on chopped parsley or green onions.

BARBECUED STEELHEAD TROUT

Grilled over coals and basted with butter sauce, trout steaks or fillets are fabulous. A touch of onion and tarragon adds to the delicate flavour. This recipe works equally well when grilled under the broiler.

4 tbsp. (60 mL)	olive oil
2 tbsp. (30 mL)	lemon juice
2 tbsp. (30 mL)	finely chopped onion, optional
2 tbsp. (30 mL)	finely chopped tarragon, optional
	salt and pepper to taste
	steelhead trout *or* salmon to serve 2, cut into steaks or fillets
4 tbsp. (60 mL)	butter, melted

Mix together the oil, juice and seasonings. Rub onto the fish. Let stand at room temperature for 1 hour for the flavours to permeate the fish.

Place fish on a greased grill 4" (10 cm) from coals that are hot to medium-hot. Cook about 6–7 minutes on each side, basting often with the melted butter. The cooking time will vary according to the heat of the coals and the thickness of the fish. If grilling under the broiler, place the fish on the rack on a baking sheet to prevent spatters in the oven.

GRILLED SWORDFISH WITH BASIL BUTTER

While waiting for this tasty dish to grill, serve an antipasto platter—they are great to nibble on before a barbeque. A slab of basil butter makes the swordfish even better!

4 tbsp. (60 mL)	unsalted butter
1 tbsp. (15 mL)	fresh lemon juice
2 tbsp. (30 mL)	finely chopped fresh basil leaves
1 tbsp. (15 mL)	finely chopped fresh chives
dash	freshly ground pepper
1/2 lb. (250 g)	swordfish steaks, per person
	black peppercorns, cracked
	oil

To make the basil butter, mix together the butter, lemon juice, herbs and pepper. Form into a log. Chill until firm.

Bring the swordfish to room temperature. Press the cracked peppercorns into both sides of the meat. Let stand a few minutes before grilling. Brush the hot grill with oil. Place the swordfish on the grill. Sear well on each side, about 3 minutes. Turn down the heat or raise the grill. Continue cooking for about 4–5 minutes on each side, or until the flesh is firm to the touch. To test, cut into the centre of the meat. It should be white and juicy looking.

Serve each swordfish steak with a thick slice of the basil butter. (Freeze any leftover basil butter for future use. It is also great with snapper or sole.)

FISH FILLETS WITH PEPPERS AND ONIONS

To add exciting colour and flavour to this dish of fresh or frozen fillets, serve with Broccoli with Pine Nuts and Tomatoes. Use halibut, cod, snapper or sole for best results.

1	small green bell pepper, thinly sliced
1	small onion, thinly sliced
2 tbsp. (30 mL)	oil
2	medium fish fillets
1- 7.5 oz. (213 mL)	tomato sauce
1 tbsp. (15 mL)	fresh lemon juice
2 tsp. (10 mL)	Worcestershire sauce
dash	hot liquid pepper

In a medium skillet, gently sauté the green pepper and onion in oil. Remove the vegetables with a slotted spoon and set aside. In the same skillet, sauté the fillets on both sides until golden. Scatter the peppers and onions over top. Mix together the tomato sauce, lemon juice, Worcestershire and hot pepper. Pour over all.

Cover and simmer for 10 minutes, or until fish is flaky but moist.

GRILLED FILLET WITH CRAB

You can substitute chicken for fish, but the cooking time will be a few minutes longer. Remove the tenderloin and save for another dish. Ovenproof your skillet by wrapping the handle in several layers of foil.

2 tbsp. (30 mL)	diced yellow pepper
2 tbsp. (30 mL)	diced red pepper
2 tbsp. (30 mL)	diced zucchini
2 oz. (60 g)	crab meat *or* imitation crab
1 tbsp. (15 mL)	dry bread crumbs
2 tsp. (10 mL)	chopped fresh dill, parsley *or* chives
2 tsp. (10 mL)	Dijon mustard (may need a bit more)
	salt and pepper to taste
2	medium fillets of red snapper *or* 2 chicken breast halves, boned and skinned, with tenderloin removed
1 tbsp. (15 mL)	each, butter and oil

Mix together all the ingredients except the fish or chicken, the butter and oil. Moisten with enough mustard to lightly bind the mixture together. Divide mixture between the fillets and press onto the top of each.

Heat the butter and oil in a skillet. Cook the fish, plain side down, for 4–5 minutes over medium heat. Place the skillet under a preheated grill. Cook 3" (7.5 cm) away from the heat for another 4–5 minutes, or until the crab mixture is golden and the fish is cooked through.

Place on a serving plate and brush with any butter left in the pan.

FILLET OF FISH EN PAPILLOTE

Red snapper is a good fish for this dish. Serve the golden, puffy paper package right from the oven. When you tear it open, enjoy the minty aromas that rise up from it. Serve with Stuffed Green Bell Peppers.

2	sheets of parchment *or* foil, about 14" x 16" (35 cm x 40 cm), folded in half and cut into a heart shape
	oil to brush on the parchment
2	medium fillets of red snapper
1 tbsp. (15 mL)	mayonnaise
1 tbsp. (15 mL)	sour cream
2 tsp. (10 mL)	fresh mint, chopped
1	tomato, cut into thin wedges
	fresh ground pepper

Open each heart-shaped sheet and brush generously with oil. Place a fillet of fish on one side of each heart. Blend together the mayonnaise and sour cream. Top each fillet with 1/2 the mayonnaise mixture, 1 tsp. (5 mL) mint, 1/2 the tomato and fresh ground pepper to taste. Fold the other side of the heart over the fillet. Crimp tightly around the edges.

Bake at 425° F (220° C) for 15 minutes, or until paper is puffed and golden.

MARINATED SHARK

Shark and swordfish absorb marinades well. Try this tasty Mexican-influenced marinade—and reserve some of it to baste the fish while it's grilling. Spaghetti Squash with Sun-Dried Tomatoes and Wild Mushrooms makes a good side dish.

1/2 lb. (250 g)	shark steak, per person
	juice of 3 limes
1/2 cup (125 mL)	olive oil (NOT strongly flavoured extra-virgin)
3/4 cup (175 mL)	finely chopped fresh cilantro
4 tbsp. (60 mL)	soft unsalted butter
	lime wedges and chopped cilantro for garnish

Place the fish in a shallow glass bowl. Mix together the lime juice, olive oil and chopped cilantro. Spread over the fish. Marinate for at least 30 minutes, turning occasionally.

Grill the fish, basting with marinade until done.

Spread butter over the steaks. Decorate with lime wedges and sprinkle with cilantro for garnish.

STEAMED CLAMS

The most common commercially-sold Pacific clams are the butter and littleneck varieties. Manila and razor clams are popular with diggers and may also be found for sale. Geoducks (pronounced gooey-ducks) are so large that they are cut into steaks. For this recipe, buy small clams in the shell either fresh or frozen.

18 - 24	clams per person, depending on size and appetites
	water
	wine, optional
1	small onion, diced
3	celery stalks, diced
	melted butter

To prepare fresh clams, scrub well and rinse one by one under cold running water. Or put them in a large pot, cover with fresh cold sea water and let stand for several hours. Then rinse in cool water. (Frozen clams are sold pre-washed and can go directly from the freezer to the cooking pot.) Discard any clams that are open. Add cornmeal to the soaking water to help get rid of sand in the shells.

If you have a special steamer, put the clams in the top with 2" (5 cm) of salted cold water in the bottom. If not, put 2" (5 cm) salted cold water in a large pot or kettle with a secure lid and add the clams. Cover.

For a more flavourful broth in which to steam the clams, add wine or half wine and water. Add the onion and celery. When the liquid comes to a rolling boil, steam just until the clams open, about 3–5 minutes.

Cook carefully. Do not overcook or the clams will be rubbery and tough. Discard any that remain closed. Drain off the broth. Strain if desired and serve in bowls (the broth is an excellent finishing touch to this dish). Serve each dinner with a bowl of melted butter.

To eat, dip each clam morsel first in the broth, then in the melted butter. Drink the broth from a mug or from the bowl.

Note: If you are digging for clams on the West Coast, always obtain the Schedule 1 Guide to safe digging areas from a Department of Fisheries and Oceans office.

PASTA

Even Italians don't know how many shapes pasta comes in. Some even have two names, depending on which part of the country you are in. Happily, pasta is no longer a heavy dish—light sauces, vegetables and seafood have made it a meal in itself.

Calzone is an unusual and tasty dish. It is a pizza filled with fresh tomato sauce, sliced smoked sausages and cheeses, then folded in half like a turnover. Gently fried or baked in a hot oven, it is eaten with a glass of cider and enthusiasm!

QUICK AND EASY PIZZA

When you use a frozen pizza crust, you can bake a pizza in less time than it takes to have one delivered!

Spread spaghetti sauce, pizza sauce or homemade salsa over the crust. Add shredded mozzarella cheese and then pick your toppings from the list below.

chopped tomatoes

sliced olives

crumbled bacon *or* ham

cooked crumbled ground beef

sliced artichokes

sliced onion *or* peppers

drained tuna *or* salmon

sliced hot dogs *or* sausage

cheddar *or* Parmesan cheese

herbs

spicy peppers

Bake at 450° F (230° C) directly on the oven rack or on a preheated baking sheet for approximately 15 minutes, or until the cheese is bubbling.

CALZONE

Shaped like turnovers and filled with the usual pizza ingredients, these calzone are gently fried in olive oil until golden. Traditionally, they are baked in very hot brick ovens. Serve hot with a salad or as a snack with wine.

Dough

1 1/4 cups (300 mL)	warm water
1 tbsp. (15 mL)	sugar
2 tbsp. (30 mL)	oil
1 tbsp. (15 mL)	yeast
3 cups (750 mL)	white all purpose flour, more or less

Place the water in a medium-sized bowl. Stir in the sugar and oil. Sprinkle on the yeast. Let stand until bubbly. Stir to mix. Whisk in the flour, 1 cup (250 mL) at a time, until the dough pulls away from the sides of the bowl and forms a ball. Add flour until the dough is no longer sticky.

Turn dough out onto a board and knead until smooth. Place in a greased bowl. Let rise for 1 hour, or until it doubles in bulk. Punch down. Divide into four 9" (22 cm) circles. Fill with some of the fillings suggested below. Fold over and crimp the edges with a fork or a pastry wheel. Fry until golden in oil heated to about 350° F (180° C).

Fillings

tomato sauce (homemade spaghetti sauce is best)

fresh *or* dried oregano, basil *or* marjoram

salt and pepper

mozzarella *or* Monterey Jack cheese, thinly sliced or shredded

anything else you like: blanched green peppers, salami, pepperoni, anchovies, olives, sautéed onion *or* sausage

FETTUCINE ALLA CARBONARA

This recipe makes four small servings for a first course or two servings for a main dish. Follow with a simple green salad and Pesche Ripiene. Use the quick Egg Pasta recipe.

2 tbsp. (30 mL)	butter
2	eggs
2 tbsp. (30 mL)	whipping cream
4 oz. (125 g)	bacon, cut up
1/2 lb. (250 g)	fettucine *or* linguine
1/2 cup (125 mL)	freshly grated Parmesan cheese
	freshly ground pepper
2 tbsp. (30 mL)	snipped parsley

Let butter, eggs and cream stand at room temperature 2–3 hours. Cook bacon until browned and crisp. Remove and drain on towelling.

Warm a serving dish. Bring a large amount of water to the boil. Add fettucine. If it is freshly made, cook for only 1–2 minutes. If it is home-made, but dried or frozen, cook for 4 minutes. If it is store bought, cook about 15 minutes. Sample a bite. It should be tender but still slightly firm. Drain thoroughly in colander. Do not rinse.

While pasta is cooking, beat together eggs and cream until just blended. Assemble other ingredients and utensils on tray. Turn pasta into the heated serving dish. At the table, toss pasta with the butter. Pour the egg mixture over pasta and toss until pasta is well coated. Add the bacon, Parmesan, pepper and parsley. Toss to mix. Serve immediately.

EGG PASTA

This homemade pasta recipe for two is quickly made in the food processor. It is best made in a processor, but a mixer will do.

2	eggs
1 1/2 cup (375 mL)	flour

Place eggs in the bowl. Start with 3/4 cup (175 mL) of the flour and mix for a few seconds. Add the balance of flour. Mix until the dough forms a ball. Add a little more flour if necessary, but do not exceed 3/4 cups (175 mL) of flour per egg. Remove from bowl and knead a few times by hand. Dough should be smooth and silky. Allow dough to rest 1 hour.

Use the pasta machine and follow the manufacturer's instructions to roll out the dough and cut into noodles.

PESTO GENOVESE

*A basic recipe for pesto is a must in every kitchen. Stir into your own home-
made Egg Pasta. Pesto freezes well, so make lots for a taste of summer on dark
winter days.*

2 cups (500 mL)	packed fresh basil *or* parsley *or* combination of parsley and basil
2	cloves garlic
4 tbsp. (60 mL)	pine nuts
1 cup (250 mL)	olive oil, more or less
	salt and pepper to taste
1/2 cup (125 mL)	Parmesan cheese

Place the basil in a food processor. Pulse 2–3 times. With machine
running, add the garlic and pine nuts. Very slowly, drizzle in the olive
oil. One cup (250 mL) is usually enough. Season to taste. Add Parmesan
cheese just before serving.

VEGETABLES AND PESTO FETTUCINE

*Light green butter lettuce in a spicy vinaigrette makes a nice complement to this
flavourful pasta dish. Madeleines and coffee are a great ending for this great
meal.*

1/2 lb. (250 g)	fettucine
2 tbsp. (30 mL)	Pesto Genovese, page 104, or to taste
1 tbsp. (15 mL)	butter
1/2 cup (125 mL)	fresh broccoli florets
3	slices onion
3 - 4	fresh mushrooms, sliced
1	small tomato, quartered
1/2 cup (125 mL)	whipping cream *or* half and half cream
2 tbsp. (30 m)	grated Romano cheese
2 tbsp. (30 mL)	grated Parmesan cheese

Cook fettucine in a large quantity of boiling water. Drain well. Toss with
the Pesto Sauce. Set aside.

Combine the butter, broccoli and onion in a small microproof bowl.
Microwave on HIGH (100%) 1–2 minutes, or until almost tender. Stir in
the mushrooms and tomato. Microwave on HIGH (100%) for 1 minute.
Remove from the microwave. Stir in the cream and cheese.

Toss the vegetable mixture with the pasta and serve immediately.

PASTA WITH PRAWNS

Tiger prawns are large and striped—and delicious! Small cooked shrimp can be substituted, if desired. Serve this dish with warm Baguette or Garlic Bread and end the dinner with a cool Yummy Parfait.

3/4 cup (175 mL)	whipping cream
4 - 6	tiger prawns
	Egg Pasta, page 103
	Parmesan cheese
	parsley

In a medium saucepan, bring the cream to a boil. Cook until slightly thickened. Add 4–6 cooked tiger prawns. Stir to coat the prawns well. Place the cooked pasta in a large serving bowl. Toss with the prawn mixture. Garnish with the cheese and parsley.

Variations: After tossing the pasta with the cream, add your favourites from this list: caviar, sun-dried tomatoes, pitted black olives, green onions, tiny shrimp, cooked meats, chicken, canned fish, cooked vegetables, fresh herbs, clams, mussels, canned or homemade salsa.

Top with Parmesan and serve.

LASAGNE

Lasagne for one or two is a snap to make in the microwave. Serve this version with Salata (Greek Salad) for a romantic Mediterranean meal.

2	lasagne noodles
1/4 lb. (125 g)	ground beef
1 tbsp. (15 mL)	chopped onion
1	clove garlic, minced
1/2 cup (125 mL)	tomato sauce
2 tbsp. (30 mL)	tomato paste
1/2 tsp. (2 mL)	freshly ground pepper
pinch	each, dried oregano and basil
4 tbsp. (60 mL)	creamed cottage cheese
4 tbsp. (60 mL)	shredded mozzarella cheese
2 tbsp. (30 mL)	grated Parmesan cheese

Cook lasagne in large quantity of boiling water. Drain. Set out flat on foil or waxed paper.

While lasagne is cooking, place ground beef, onion and garlic in a 1 qt. (1 L) microproof bowl. Microwave on HIGH (100%) for 1–3 minutes, or until all the pink in the meat is gone. Drain off fat. Stir in the tomato sauce, paste, pepper and herbs. Microwave on HIGH (100%) for 4 minutes, or until heated through and flavours are blended. Stir occasionally. Remove from microwave.

In a small bowl, combine the cheeses. Reserve 1/2 cup (125 mL) of the beef mixture. Spread the remaining mixture down the centre of each lasagne noodle. Top with half the cheese mixture. Roll up the lasagne. Place, seam side down, in a small microproof casserole. Top with reserved meat mixture and the remaining cheese. Cover.

Microwave on MEDIUM (50%) or MEDIUM HIGH (80%) until the rolls are heated through and the cheese melts. Rotate the dish half a turn at half time. Let stand 5 minutes before serving.

Opposite: Quick and Easy Pizza.

VEGETABLES

Fresh, fresh, fresh ingredients, straight from the marketplace into the pot, mean you'll never have a failed vegetable dish. I have touched on only a few types in this book. Remember the seasons, and shop for asparagus in the spring. Buy corn in August and pop it into a pot of boiling water for a few minutes. Top with butter and pepper and eat right away. Roll the asparagus or corn in one of the vinaigrettes for a tasty change. Serve warm or at room temperature.

VEGETABLE FRITTERS

While fritters are usually deep-fried, these ones cook just as well in a skillet. They are wonderful with a steak. Grill the meat while you cook the vegetables, and they should be done at the same time.

2	eggs
1 cup (250 mL)	vegetables: finely grated carrot, zucchini, onion, julienne snow peas, red pepper, cooked corn kernels
1	medium potato, peeled and grated
2 tbsp. (30 mL)	flour
	salt and pepper
2 tbsp. (30 mL)	butter
1 tbsp. (15 mL)	oil

Beat the eggs. Place the grated carrot, zucchini and onion in a strainer over a bowl. Press out the excess juices (or whirl in a lettuce spinner or place in a tea towel and wring out the moisture). Mix together with the rest of the vegetables. Stir in the eggs. Mix in the flour, salt and pepper.

In a medium skillet, melt the butter and oil. Divide the vegetable mixture into 3 or 4 servings. Spoon into the pan and form into pancakes. Fry over medium heat until crisp and golden, about 3 minutes. Turn and fry on the other side.

The fritters can be kept warm for about 5–10 minutes in a low oven, but are best served immediately.

SAUTÉ OF GREEN BEANS

2 tbsp. (30 mL)	butter
1	medium sweet onion, finely chopped
1	medium tomato, seeded and coarsely chopped
	salt
1/2 tsp. (2 mL)	oregano
3/4 lb. (375 g)	green beans, parboiled 12–15 minutes (still slightly firm) and drained well
	pepper
	chopped parsley

In a medium skillet, melt 1 tbsp. (15 mL) of the butter. Add the onion and gently sauté until tender.

In a separate pan, stew the tomatoes in the remaining butter with a pinch of salt and oregano. Toss to prevent sticking until nearly dry.

Add the beans to the onions. Salt them. Cook over medium heat, stirring occasionally, for about 10–15 minutes, or until beans are tender. Add the tomatoes, pepper and some parsley. Toss all together until heated through. Sprinkle with the remaining parsley and serve.

MINTED SNOW PEAS

15 - 20	frozen *or* fresh snow peas
1 tbsp. (15 mL)	butter
	fresh mint, if possible, *or* Spice Islands Garden Mint

Bring a pot of water to the boil. Drop in the snow peas. Boil for 1 minute. Drain and rinse under cold water. Pat dry.

Melt butter in a skillet. Stir-fry snow peas until heated through. Season with the mint. Serve immediately.

CASSEROLE PEAS

2 tbsp. (30 mL)	butter
4 oz. (125 g)	fresh mushrooms, sliced
1- 300 g pkg.	frozen peas
1- 10 oz. (284 mL) can	mushroom soup
1/2- 8 oz. (227 mL) can	water chestnuts, drained and sliced
	toasted slivered almonds *or* french fried onion rings for garnish

Melt the butter in a medium skillet. Add the mushrooms. Sauté for 4–5 minutes until tender. Drain. Combine with the peas, soup and water chestnuts in a medium casserole.

Bake at 350° F (180° C) for 20–25 minutes, or until heated through and bubbling. Top with the almonds or onion rings. Return to the oven to brown.

CARROTS VICHY

Carrots give a good deal of colour to a dinner plate and this dish makes a cheerful complement to any meal. "Vichy" is a cooking method known as "sweating", in which foil is pressed right down on the vegetable, which is then gently cooked in a covered pan.

2 tbsp. (30 mL)	butter
pinch	sugar
2 - 4	medium carrots, finely sliced or julienned
1 tbsp. (15 mL)	cognac *or* brandy
	Dijon Sauce, recipe follows
2 tbsp. (30 mL)	fine dry bread crumbs
1 tbsp. (15 mL)	chopped chives

Melt the butter in a small baking dish. Stir in the sugar. Add carrots and cognac. Place foil over the carrots, pressing down to cover well. Cover pan with more foil or a lid.

Bake at 350° F (180° C) for 1 hour. Do not stir during baking but check now and then to make sure carrots do not burn. Add more butter, if necessary.

Remove foil from carrots. Pour over Dijon Sauce. Sprinkle on bread crumbs and chives. Bake 10 minutes more.

Dijon Sauce

1/2 cup (125 mL)	sour cream
1 tbsp. (15 mL)	Dijon mustard
1 tbsp. (15 mL)	white all purpose flour
pinch	sugar
1/2 cup (125 mL)	liquid from baked carrots and water to make 1/2 cup (125 mL)
	pepper to taste

Stir together the sour cream, mustard, flour and sugar. Gradually stir in the hot liquid from the carrots to form a thick sauce. You may not need the total 1/2 cup (125 mL) of the liquid. Season to taste.

CELERY ROOT JULIENNE

Celery root is a large bulbous root with a faint celery-like flavour. Available in the fall, it is a nice vegetable for a change of pace.

1 lb. (500 g)	celery root
2 tbsp. (30 mL)	butter
	salt
	pepper
	juice of 1 lemon
	chopped parsley

Peel the celery root. Cut in very thin julienne strips or shred coarsely. Melt the butter in a large heavy skillet. Add celery root. Sauté, tossing and stirring constantly, for 2–3 minutes.

Cover. Cook over moderate heat 5–8 minutes until tender. Add more butter, if necessary. Season with salt, pepper, lemon and parsley.

BROCCOLI WITH PINE NUTS AND TOMATOES

This is a different way to serve broccoli. The red pepper flakes add a hot tang—don't add too many!

1	small bunch of broccoli florets
2 tbsp. (30 mL)	olive oil
pinch	dried red pepper flakes
1	clove garlic, minced
3 tbsp. (45 mL)	pine nuts
1 - 2	tomatoes, seeded and chopped
pinch	salt and pepper

Parboil the broccoli in large quanity of boiling water until tender-crisp, about 5 minutes. Chill under cold running water. Set aside until serving time.

Just before serving, heat the oil in a medium skillet. Add the pepper flakes and garlic. Cook for 1–2 minutes. Add the pine nuts. Sauté over low heat until the nuts just begin to colour.

Add the broccoli. Sauté until tender and heated through, about 5 minutes. Add the tomatoes and cook another minute or two. Season to taste.

SPINACH WITH NUTS

In this dish, fresh spinach is tossed with toasted nuts.

2 tbsp. (30 mL)	butter
4 tbsp. (60 mL)	nuts, such as walnuts, pine nuts, pecans, almonds
1	bunch fresh spinach, washed and shaken dry
	salt, pepper and nutmeg

In a medium skillet, melt the butter. Sauté the nuts for 2–3 minutes, stirring occasionally. Remove the nuts and reserve.

Add the slightly damp spinach leaves. Toss to heat through, about 4 minutes. Return the nuts to the pan. Add salt, pepper and nutmeg to taste. Serve immediately.

STUFFED BELL PEPPERS

Many colours of bell peppers are available in the market—and they all taste wonderful! This recipe requires four medium-sized ones. Serve them warm, at room temperature or chilled as a first course.

2 tbsp. (30 mL)	olive oil
1	small onion, chopped
1/2 cup (125 mL)	uncooked rice
2 tbsp. (30 mL)	pine nuts
1 tbsp. (15 mL)	tomato paste
pinch	each, salt, pepper, sugar and allspice
2 tbsp. (30 mL)	chopped fresh mint *or* 2 tsp. (5 mL) dried mint
1 tbsp. (15 mL)	lemon juice
4	bell peppers, medium to small

In a medium saucepan, heat the oil. Add the onions and cook until softened. Add the rice. Cook, stirring, until grains are well coated with oil. Add the pine nuts and stir for 1 minute. Pour in 1 cup (250 mL) of hot water. Add the tomato paste, salt, pepper, sugar and allspice. Bring to a boil. Cover and reduce the heat. Simmer for 20 minutes, or until rice is tender.

Using a fork, toss the rice. Add mint and lemon juice. Toss again, mixing well. Cool.

Remove the tops from the bell peppers. Pull out the seeds and the hard white ribs. Rinse and drain. Stuff the peppers. Arrange in a casserole. Add 1 1/2 cups (375 mL) of water. Bring to a boil. Cover and simmer for 45 minutes on top of the stove or in the oven, until the peppers are tender. Cool slightly in the casserole and serve.

WARM RED CABBAGE

Lightly cooked red cabbage makes a wonderful and tasty garnish.

1/2	small head red cabbage
2 tbsp. (30 mL)	vinegar
2 tbsp. (30 mL)	olive oil
	salt and pepper to taste

Remove the core of the cabbage. Shred cabbage finely lengthwise into long strips. Place in a medium bowl.

Bring the vinegar to a boil in a medium saucepan. Pour it over the shredded cabbage. Mix well. The cabbage will turn bright red. The dish may be made ahead to this point. Keep at room temperature.

Just before serving, heat the olive oil in a large skillet. Add the cabbage and toss until heated through. Season to taste.

BAKED ONIONS

Onions become sweet and succulent when baked. In this version, balsamic vinegar adds a smoky tart flavour.

4	medium unpeeled onions
1/3 cup (75 mL)	olive oil
	salt
	freshly ground pepper
1/3 cup (75 mL)	balsamic vinegar (sherry vinegar can be substituted)

Place the onions in a small deep roasting pan. Pour the oil over top. Roll the onions in it to coat them. Bake at 375° F (190° C) for 1 1/2 hours, or until tender when pierced with a skewer.

Carefully remove to a serving dish and cut into halves. Sprinkle with salt and pepper. Stir the vinegar into the pan juices. Cook over medium heat, stirring, until slightly thickened. Spoon over onion halves and serve.

RICE PILAF (Wild Rice Casserole)

	sliced almonds
1 cup (250 mL)	wild rice
1 1/2 cups (375 mL)	beef *or* chicken broth
1 tbsp. (15 mL)	butter
3 - 4	whole green onion, chopped
3 - 4	whole fresh mushrooms, sliced

Place almonds on a baking sheet. Bake at 350° F (180° C) for about 8–10 minutes, watching carefully as they burn easily, or until lightly browned. Cool.

In a medium ovenproof casserole, mix together the rice and broth. Let stand overnight.

In a small skillet, melt the butter. Add the green onions and mushrooms. Sauté until tender, about 3–4 minutes. Stir into the rice. Cover and bake until all liquid is absorbed, about 40 minutes. It may be necessary to add a little more liquid if rice is not tender after 40 minutes. Garnish with toasted almonds.

RANCH CUT POTATOES

For this dish, choose oval, brown-skinned, Idaho-type potatoes.

2	medium potatoes
2 tbsp. (30 mL)	unsalted clarified butter, bacon drippings *or* cooking oil
	salt and pepper

Cut the potatoes lengthwise into strips about 1/2" (1 cm) thick. Soak them in cold water until baking time, if desired. Drain well. Spread in a single layer on a flat baking sheet. Pour the melted butter over and stir until well coated.

Bake at 450° F (230° C) for 30–40 minutes, turning the potato slices several times. Drain on paper towels. Season with salt and pepper, if desired.

POTATO HASH WITH RED AND GREEN PEPPERS

For quick and easy preparation of this dish, fry the potatoes ahead of time. To serve, reheat and add the red and green peppers. Cook only until heated through.

2 - 3	large potatoes, peeled and diced, about 1/4" (5 mm)
	lemon water
2 tbsp. (30 mL)	butter
2 tbsp. (30 mL)	oil
1	small red bell pepper, cored and diced, about 1/4" (5 mm)
1	small green bell pepper, cored and diced, about 1/4" (5 mm)
	additional butter *or* oil, for reheating

Peel and dice the potatoes, placing them in the lemon water to prevent browning. When all are diced, drain well and pat dry on paper towelling.

Heat the butter and oil in a large skillet. Add the potatoes. Cook, stirring and tossing, until tender and golden brown. Turn out onto paper towels to drain. Store at room temperature until serving time.

Just before serving, heat a little more butter and oil, as needed, in a large skillet. Add the potatoes and the peppers. Fry until hot through. Serve immediately.

SPAGHETTI SQUASH

Spaghetti squash is often sold by the piece in produce departments.

1	small squash, about 2 lb. (1 kg)
2 tbsp. (30 mL)	oil
1	clove garlic, chopped
	parsley for garnish

Cut squash in half and remove seeds. Place cut side down on a greased cookie sheet. Bake at 375° F (190° C) until tender when pierced with a skewer, about 45 minutes. Scrape out the meat. It will shred into spaghetti-like strands. The dish can be prepared ahead to this point.

When ready to serve, heat olive oil in a skillet. Add a chopped clove of garlic. Sauté squash until heated through. Sprinkle with parsley.

SPAGHETTI SQUASH WITH SUN-DRIED TOMATOES AND WILD MUSHROOMS

Regular tomatoes and mushrooms can be substituted with only a slight variation in flavour. Serve as a vegetable side dish.

2	large dried mushrooms, such as boletus, porcini, cep, shiitake
1	small spaghetti squash, about 2 lb. (1 kg)
2	whole sun-dried tomatoes
2 tbsp. (30 mL)	butter
2 tbsp. (30 mL)	oil

Cover the mushrooms with hot water to soften. Cut the spaghetti squash in half and remove seeds. Place the pieces cut side down on a baking sheet. Bake at 350° F (180° C) until tender when pierced with a skewer, about 45 minutes. Remove from the oven and cool slightly. Scrape out the meat of the squash (it will look like strings of fine spaghetti) and place in a bowl.

Sliver the tomatoes. Drain the mushrooms and pat dry. Discard any tough stems and sliver.

Just before serving, heat the butter and oil in a large skillet or spray with vegetable spray. Add the squash, tomatoes and mushrooms. Toss and cook until heated through.

PUMPKIN CONSERVE (Chutney)

This pumpkin chutney is delicious with meat and vegetables or on toast.
Your guests will wonder what the bright orange chunks are. The finely diced
Australian ginger in syrup adds a piquant taste. The dish can be made ahead
and kept in the refrigerator for up to 3 months. It also freezes well.
Makes 5- 8 oz. (250 mL) jars.

6 - 7 cups (1.5 - 1.75 L)	fresh pumpkin
3	lemons
1	orange
2 cups (500 mL)	raisins
3 tbsp. (45 mL)	ginger in syrup, finely chopped
4 cups (1 L)	sugar

Peel the pumpkin and dice into 1/2" (1 cm) chunks. Place in a large
bowl. Slice the citrus fruit paper thin, removing any seeds. Add the fruit,
raisins and ginger. Stir. Add the sugar and stir well.

Let stand, covered, 10–12 hours or overnight at room temperature,
stirring occasionally.

Transfer to a large saucepan. Place over medium heat. Simmer 2 1/2
hours, or until well reduced and thickened. The mixture will thicken
more upon standing. Spoon into hot sterilized jars. Cool.

EGG DISHES

Brunch or light suppers let egg dishes shine. Frittatas are open-faced omelettes, finished in the oven or under the broiler. They are dressy enough for company at any time of day. Use large eggs for all these recipes.

PRAWN FRITTATA WITH SUN-DRIED TOMATOES

In this variation of the Italian omelette, the frittata is cooked for a few minutes on the stove top, then finished under the broiler. **Makes one 8" (20 cm).**

2 tbsp. (30 mL)	olive oil
2 tbsp. (30 mL)	butter
1 lb. (500 g)	raw peeled prawns *or* shrimp
3 - 4	green onions, diagonally sliced
6	large eggs, well beaten
	a few sun-dried tomatoes, whole *or* in large chunks
	salt and pepper to taste

Turn on the oven to broil.

Heat the oil and butter in an 8" (20 cm) heavy ovenproof skillet. (If you do not have a skillet that will go in the oven, protect the handle of your regular skillet with several layers of aluminum foil.) Add the prawns and cook until just barely pink. Add the green onions and cook briefly over medium heat.

Pour the beaten eggs over everything. Cook until the egg mixture begins to look done around the edges. Lift the mixture gently from time to time at the edges to allow some of the egg mixture on top to flow underneath. This will speed up the cooking time.

As the mixture begins to firm slightly, add the tomatoes. Push them a little under the surface of the liquid. Place the pan under the broiler until the top turns a golden brown and puffs at the edges.

Remove from oven and slip onto a serving plate. Sprinkle on a little salt and pepper. Cut into wedges and serve.

Opposite: Prawn Frittata with Sun-Dried Tomatoes.

PUFFY FRITTATA

*A frittata is an open-faced omelette, made on top of the stove and finished in the oven. Serve hot or room at temperature, for brunch, lunch or supper. A frittata is always popular! Use a cast iron skillet for best results. **Makes one 8" (20 cm)**.*

1/2 cup (125 mL)	sour cream
8	eggs
2 tsp. (10 mL)	chopped fresh basil
2 tsp. (10 mL)	chopped fresh tarragon
2 tsp. (10 mL)	chopped fresh parsley
1/2 tsp. (2 mL)	salt
1/2 tsp. (2 mL)	freshly ground pepper
pinch	cayenne pepper
2 tbsp. (30 mL)	butter
4 tbsp. (60 mL)	chopped green onion, including green tops
4 - 5	whole fresh mushrooms, sliced
4 - 5	slices bacon, cooked until crisp, optional
2 - 3 tbsp. (30 - 45 mL)	grated Parmesan cheese
	tomato slices and parsley sprigs for garnish

In a large bowl, beat the sour cream until smooth. Add the eggs one at a time, beating until blended. Stir in the basil, tarragon, parsley, salt, pepper and cayenne. Set aside.

In an 8" (20 cm) skillet with an ovenproof handle, melt the butter over medium heat. Add the green onions and mushrooms. Cook, stirring, until vegetables are tender, about 5 minutes. Remove from heat. Stir in egg mixture. Crumble bacon and add to pan. Sprinkle top with cheese.

Bake frittata, uncovered, at 375° F (190° C) until puffy and set in the centre, about 20 minutes. (If you don't have a cast iron skillet or one with an ovenproof handle, wrap three or four layers of aluminum foil around the handle of your regular skillet.)

Serve the frittata hot or at room temperature, garnished with tomato slices and parsley sprigs.

VEGETABLE OMELETTE

Omelettes are best made in individual sizes. They cook quickly and can be kept warm while you whip up a second, third or fourth. Never wash your omelette pan—just wipe it clean.

If you prefer a puffy omelette, separate the eggs. Beat the egg yolks with water and fold in stiffly beaten egg whites. Many ingredients can be added before cooking. Or cook them separately and spread on the omelette before folding it. **Makes 1**.

	pre-cooked leftover vegetables, including some onion mixed with a spoonful or two of tomato catsup
	parsley, chive *or* basil, dried *or* fresh
	ham *or* cheese *or* both
2	eggs
1 tbsp. (15 mL)	water
	salt and pepper, optional
1 tbsp. (15 mL)	butter

Prepare the vegetables. Chop the fresh herbs. Julienne or dice the ham. Grate the cheese. Beat together the eggs, water and seasonings. Add the vegetables, ham, cheese and herbs, or set them aside for spreading on just before folding the omelette.

Heat the omelette pan over medium-high heat. Add the butter, which should immediately sizzle and melt. Pour on the egg mixture. Cook until almost set but still very slightly runny on top. If filling has not been added, spread it on now. Slip the omelette onto a warmed serving platter, folding the top half over the bottom as it slides out of the pan.

EASY OMELETTE WITH SALSA

Omelettes are fast and easy. Add any topping that you have handy—sweet or savoury. Serve with toast and tea. **Makes 1.**

1 tbsp. (15 mL)	butter
2	eggs, lightly beaten
1 tbsp. (15 mL)	water
	chopped fresh herbs for a savoury omelette
	salt and pepper, optional
	salsa, jam *or* jelly for garnish

In an 8" (20 cm) non-stick skillet, melt the butter. Mix the eggs and water. Pour into the hot pan. Reduce the heat to medium. Cook, lifting the edges slightly with a spatula. When the mixture starts to set on top, scatter on the herbs, salt and pepper. Cook a few seconds more.

Slide the omelette onto a warmed serving plate, folding one half over the other (this requires a little practice). Garnish with salsa, jam or jelly. Serve immediately.

ZUCCHINI QUICHE

This quiche is wonderful for brunch or lunch with sliced tomatoes. It's also very nice at room temperature and great the next day. Make your own pastry from your favourite recipe or buy a package of frozen dough. Instead of the zucchini, add chopped, cooked broccoli, carrots, onions or spinach for a change of pace.
Makes one 8" (20 cm).

1	unbaked pie crust
3 tbsp. (45 mL)	butter
1	onion, thinly sliced
2	zucchini
3	eggs
3/4 cup (175 mL)	sour cream
1 tsp. (5 mL)	Dijon mustard
pinch	each, nutmeg, basil, salt and pepper
1 cup (250 mL)	grated Swiss cheese

Heat oven to 425° F (220° C). Roll out pastry and place in an 8" (20 cm) pie pan or quiche dish. Make a high rim and lightly prick bottom and sides. Chill.

Cover pastry with foil and fill with baking beans. Bake in oven for 8 minutes. Remove foil and beans. Bake a further few minutes until crust is lightly golden. Remove from oven and allow to cool. Reduce heat to 350° F (180° C).

Melt butter in a large skillet. Add onion and cook over medium heat until lightly browned. Stir often. In the food processor using the french fry blade or coarse shredder, cut the zucchini into thin julienne strips. Add to the onions. Cook, stirring constantly, for about 3–4 minutes. Drain well on paper towels.

In a large bowl, beat the eggs with the sour cream, mustard and seasonings until well mixed. Stir in the cheese, zucchini and onions. Pour into baked pie shell. Bake for 30–40 minutes, or until a knife inserted slightly off-centre comes out clean. Let stand for 5 minutes before cutting.

DIANE'S PUFF PANCAKE

My daughter likes to entertain at brunch and often serves this pancake, which is like a popover. Quick and easy, it will bake while you welcome your guest.

If you don't have a cast iron skillet, wrap two or three layers of foil around the handle of your regular skillet to protect it in the oven, or use a well-greased cake tin.

This recipe makes a hearty pancake for one. To serve two, double everything but the eggs and bake in two pans. To serve three, triple everything but use only three eggs. Serve with a sprinkling of icing sugar and top with fruit or jam.

1/2 cup (125 mL)	milk, at room temperature
1 tsp. (5 mL)	vanilla
pinch	nutmeg
2	eggs, at room temperature
1/2 cup (125 mL)	white all purpose flour
	butter
1 tbsp. (15 mL)	icing sugar
	fruit *or* jam

Beat together the milk, vanilla, nutmeg and eggs. Whisk in the flour. The batter will be lumpy.

Heat the oven to 400° F (200° C). Lightly butter an 8" (20 cm) cast iron skillet. Heat pan in the oven (do not burn the butter). Pour on the batter. If you are baking 2 or 3 pancakes, use 1 cup of batter for each. Bake each pancake for 15 minutes, or until well puffed and golden.

When the pancake is removed from the oven, the centre will slump in. This is a perfect place to sprinkle the sugar and top with the fruit or jam. Serve immediately.

NOUVELLE FRENCH TOAST

A tasty light version of the French Toast Sandwich, this recipe makes a great luncheon dish. It is even more delicious if the egg and milk mixture has 2 tbsp. (30 mL) of maple syrup added to it. **Serves 2**.

4 - 6	large ripe strawberries
4 slices	French bread
3 1/2 oz. (100 g)	Brie *or* Camembert
2	eggs
2 tbsp. (30 mL)	milk
pinch	nutmeg
	butter
	syrup

Slice 2–3 of the strawberries, reserving the whole ones for the garnish. Spread 2 slices of bread with the cheese. Top with the sliced strawberries. Cover with another slice of bread.

Lightly beat the eggs, milk and nutmeg in a large flat container. Place the sandwiches into the egg mixture and let stand for a few minutes. Turn and let the other sides of the sandwiches soak up the remainder of the egg mixture.

Heat a lightly buttered skillet over medium heat. Add the sandwiches and fry until golden brown on each side.

Serve with whole strawberries and warmed syrup.

FRENCH TOAST SANDWICH

On restaurant menus, this type of sandwich is often called a Monte Cristo. This recipe makes a quick, light dinner. Take the second one with you for lunch the next day—it tastes great cold! **Makes 2**.

4 slices	bread
2 slices	cheese
2 slices	corned beef
2	eggs
1 tbsp. (15 mL)	milk
	butter
	syrup
	freshly ground pepper

Cover 2 slices of bread with the cheese and beef. Top with the remaining bread. Lightly beat the eggs, milk and pepper. Place the sandwiches into the egg mixture. Let stand for a few minutes. Turn and let the other side of the sandwiches soak up the remainder of the egg mixture.

Heat a lightly buttered skillet over medium heat. Add the sandwiches and fry until golden brown on each side.

Serve with warmed syrup and freshly ground pepper.

DESSERTS AND DRINKS

My favourite part of the meal is dessert! I found designing desserts for just two people to be challenging. Cakes and pies are for a crowd, and they go stale in the fridge, waiting to be eaten. But try making a pie crust in small 4" (10 cm) pie pans found in specialty kitchen shops, and add your favorite filling. Bake one for the two of you and freeze the others for another day. Cake recipes can be baked in muffin tins, making cupcakes that can be frozen easily. Baking time is reduced to about 15 or 20 minutes. Balls of cookie dough freeze easily. Bake a few right from the freezer when a cookie attack hits. Allow an extra five minutes in the oven.

A drink before dinner, with or without an appetizer, will relax you after the stresses of the day. The two Sangrias and Lemonade recipes make larger quantities. Keep them refrigerated, and just top them up with soda in a tall glass when you are ready for them. They will keep for several weeks.

CHOCOLATE VALENTINE'S CAKE

Make this cake in a heart-shaped cake tin and ice with Pink Peppermint Valentine Frosting. Don't wait for Valentine's Day—serve any time of year!

2 tbsp. (30 mL)	butter, melted and cooled
1/2 cup (125 mL)	white all purpose flour
1/2 cup (125 mL)	unsweetened cocoa
3	large eggs, at room temperature
1/2 cup (125 mL)	granulated sugar
	liqueur

With some of the melted butter, lightly grease a 9" (23 cm) or heart-shaped cake pan.

Mix together flour and cocoa. Set aside. In a medium bowl, beat the eggs and sugar until light and thick, and the mixture forms a ribbon when the beaters are raised, about 5 minutes.

Sift the flour and cocoa into the egg mixture (a strainer makes a good sifter). Stir in quickly with a few strokes. Add the remaining melted butter and finish folding. Spread into the cake pan.

Bake at 350° F (180° C) for 15–20 minutes. The cake is done when it springs back to the touch. Remove the cake before it shrinks from the sides of the pan, because it will be overdone by then.

Turn out immediately onto a cake rack and cool. The bottom side is the right side. Split the cake in half, if desired. Sprinkle with a favourite liqueur before icing. The cake may be made ahead to this point and frozen.

Pink Peppermint Valentine Frosting

This recipe fills and ices one 9" (23 cm) cake. It can be refrigerated until serving time and also freezes well.

1 tsp. (5 mL)	unflavoured gelatin
2 tbsp. (30 mL)	cold water
2 tbsp. (30 mL)	sugar
1/2 tsp. (2 mL)	peppermint extract
1 cup (250 mL)	whipping cream, chilled
2 drops	red food colouring

In a small pot, soften the gelatin in the cold water. Dissolve it over low heat. Cool to room temperature.

Meanwhile, add the sugar and peppermint extract to the cream. Beat it until it begins to thicken. Slowly pour in the dissolved gelatin. Add the food colouring and continue beating until thick. Spread the whipping cream evenly over the cake layers. Cover completely and swirl a decorative design on the surface. Do this immediately, before the gelatin sets.

FRUIT COMPOTE

Serve this compote over ice cream with Madeleines on the side. Vary the fruit to suit the season.

3 tbsp. (45 mL)	sugar
2 tbsp. (30 mL)	water
	zest of 2 oranges
3 tbsp. (45 mL)	Irish Mist Liqueur, optional
2	oranges, peeled and sectioned
1	kiwi fruit, peeled and sliced

Combine the sugar, water and orange zest in a small saucepan. Slowly cook until sugar dissolves. Bring to a boil. Reduce heat and cook for 3–4 minutes. Set aside.

When cool, stir in the liqueur, if desired. Pour over the fruit. Marinate for at least 1 hour.

MADELEINES

These dainty, airy cakes take their name from the special shape of the pan they are baked in. Plan to eat them the day they are made, because they do not keep well. If there are any leftovers, make them into crumbs and use in Pesche Ripiene. **Makes 18.**

3 tbsp. (45 mL)	butter, melted
3	large eggs
1/3 cup (75 mL)	sugar
1/4 tsp. (1 mL)	vanilla
1/2 cup (125 mL)	white all purpose flour
	icing sugar

With some of the melted butter, lightly brush the baking tins. Shake a bit of the sugar into them, which will form a coat to make the outside of the madeleine crispy when baked.

Beat eggs with sugar until they are thick and light, and a ribbon forms when the beater is raised, about 5 minutes. Stir in the vanilla. Shake the flour through a sieve onto the batter. Quickly stir it in. Add the butter rapidly.

Drop by large spoonfuls into the madeleine pans. Bake until light brown, about 10–15 minutes. Remove from pans and turn shell side up. Sprinkle with icing sugar.

OLD-FASHIONED STRAWBERRY SHORTCAKE WITH DEVON-STYLE CREAM

Delicate little biscuits filled with homemade Devon-Style Cream and a generous number of strawberries yield a rich dessert, so don't make the shortcakes too large. The shortcakes freeze well until ready to eat. Thaw at room temperature or for 30 seconds on HIGH in your microwave. The cream will keep for four or five days in the refrigerator.

6 tbsp. (90 mL)	soft butter
4 tbsp. (60 mL)	sugar
1/2 cup (125 mL)	sour cream
1	egg
1 1/2 cups (375 mL)	white all purpose flour
2 tsp. (10 mL)	baking powder
1/2 tsp. (2 mL)	salt
1/4 tsp. (1 mL)	baking soda
1 qt. (1 L)	strawberries, or as many as needed for each shortcake
1 cup (250 mL)	Devon-Style Cream, recipe follows

Cream the butter and sugar until smooth. Beat in the sour cream and egg. Mix together the flour, baking powder, salt and baking soda. Stir into butter mixture. Stir until just moistened. Turn the mixture onto a floured board. Pat into a circle about 1/2" (1 cm) thick. With a medium-sized glass or round cutter, cut out circles and place on a greased baking sheet. Gently reform and pat the dough until it is all used. There should be 8 rounds. Bake at 400° F (200° C) for 12–15 minutes, or until golden brown. Cool on a wire rack. The dish may be made ahead to this point and frozen.

Carefully split the shortcakes. Fill with strawberries and cream. Top with additional cream and one large strawberry for a dramatic garnish!

Devon-Style Cream

1 cup (250 mL)	whipping cream
2 tbsp. (30 mL)	light brown sugar
1/2 cup (125 mL)	sour cream

In a small bowl, combine the whipping cream and sugar. Stir to dissolve. Whip the mixture until soft peaks form. Fold in the sour cream. Refrigerate for several hours to allow flavours to blend.

SEASONAL FRUIT WITH ROSEWATER

Rosewater is used a great deal in the cooking of southern France. It is readily available in the baking section of most markets. This dish will keep in the refrigerator for up to three days.

1/2	small honeydew melon
1	cantaloupe
1	pomegranate, optional
	a handful of green grapes
2	medium nectarines
1/2 cup (125 mL)	sugar
5 tbsp. (75 mL)	lemon juice
5 tbsp. (75 mL)	rosewater
	finely chopped pistachio nuts, optional
sprinkling	cinnamon, optional

Peel melons. Cut into cubes or make balls with melon baller. Put balls in a deep bowl. Pour any melon juice over. Add pomegranate seeds and its juices and grapes. Slice the nectarines thinly. Add to melon. Add remaining ingredients, except nuts and cinnamon, and gently mix. Cover tightly and refrigerate for at least 2 hours.

Garnish with pistachio nuts and cinnamon, if desired.

STRAWBERRY MERINGUES

There's no need to wait for the strawberry season to try this wonderful dessert. Use fresh raspberries, blackberries, peaches or nectarines. Or be adventuresome with some of the fruits from New Zealand!

6 oz. (180 g)	milk chocolate (try Belgian *or* Swiss *or* a good chocolate bar)
1 tbsp. (15 mL)	brandy
1 cup (250 mL)	whipping cream
	sugar to taste
1 tsp. (5 mL)	vanilla
4	meringues (available at bakeries)
	fresh strawberries

Gently melt the chocolate with the brandy. Set aside to cool.

Whip the cream. Add the sugar to taste. Fold in the vanilla. Place 2 meringues on individual dessert plates. Gently spread on a little melted chocolate. Mound on some whipped cream. Top with sliced or whole fresh strawberries.

Refrigerate for up to 2 hours to allow the meringue to mellow slightly and become a little chewy.

ORANGES JUBILEE

Serve this variation of cherries jubilee to your best friend after a dinner of Rack of Lamb for Two or Simmered Chicken.

2 tbsp. (30 mL)	sugar
2 tbsp. (30 mL)	butter
	grated zest of 1 small orange
	grated zest of 1 small lemon
	juice of 1 small orange
	juice of 1 small lemon
2 - 4 tbsp. (30 - 60 mL)	cointreau *or* other orange liqueur
2	oranges, peeled and sectioned, *or* fruit of your choice
2	large scoops vanilla ice cream
2 - 4 tbsp. (30 - 60 mL)	brandy

In a heavy medium saucepan (or small electric skillet at the table), heat sugar over medium-high heat. Without stirring, cook until sugar dissolves and turns slightly caramel in colour. Stir in butter. Add zest and juices. Stir well.

Add orange liqueur and cook 5 minutes over medium heat. Add fruit and heat through. Place ice cream in dessert dishes. (If prepared in the kitchen to this point, take pan to table and continue.)

Warm brandy in a small container. Stand well back and ignite the brandy with a long match. Pour into skillet over fruit mixture, stirring to help flame. Spoon flaming fruit and sauce over ice cream.

Opposite: Old-Fashioned Strawberry Shortcake with Devon-Style Cream.

FRESH NECTARINES WITH CREAM CHEESE IN A RASPBERRY SAUCE

This recipe make a luscious summer dessert. But you can serve it any time, because nectarines seem to be available almost all year round. Blueberries, cherries and grapes can be substituted for the raspberries.

2	perfect medium nectarines
1/2 cup (125 mL)	creamed cheese, such as Winnipeg cream cheese
	lemon juice, optional
1 cup (250 mL)	fresh raspberries
	raspberry liqueur *or* a liqueur of your choice
	icing sugar, optional

Slice the fruit in half and carefuly remove the pits. Form some of the cream cheese into a ball a little larger than the pit. Place in one half of the fruit. If you are not serving the dish immediately, brush the fruit with some lemon juice.

Purée the raspberries. Press through a strainer to remove some of the seeds. Stir in a little liqueur and taste for sweetness. Add some icing sugar, if necessary.

At serving time, spoon some of the purée into the centre of a dessert plate. Place the half of the fruit with the cream cheese on the plate. Place the other half slightly overlapped on top.

For an alternative, slice the fruit and fan the slices out. Place some of the cream cheese to one side. Serve chilled.

BANANA SOUFFLÉ FLAMBÉ

This dramatic presentation definitely needs an audience! The dish will stay hot enough to light the brandy at the table.

1 tbsp. (15 mL)	butter
2 - 3	medium bananas, sliced and sprinkled with juice of 1/2 lemon
1/2 cup (125 mL)	sugar
4	egg yolks
4	egg whites, beaten until soft peaks form
	icing sugar
2 - 4 tbsp. (30 - 60 mL)	cognac, brandy *or* rum, at room temperature

Heat oven to 400° F (200° C). Butter an ovenproof serving platter with slanted sides (to prevent the flambé mixture from overflowing).

Melt the butter in a medium skillet. Add the banana slices and 2 tbsp. (30 mL) of the sugar. Sauté for 3–4 minutes. Set aside.

Beat together the rest of the sugar and egg yolks for 2–3 minutes. Fold the beaten egg whites into the sugar and egg mixture. Spread 1/3 of this mixture into the prepared serving dish. Bake in the oven for 5 minutes.

Remove from oven and arrange the sautéed bananas over the cooked portion. Cover with the remaining mixture. Bake for 6–8 minutes more, or until puffed and golden.

Remove from oven and sprinkle on a little icing sugar. Take to the table. Pour over the cognac. Stand well back and ignite with a long match. Serve immediately.

PESCHE RIPIENE

This famous Italian dessert can be multiplied to serve any number of guests.
Serve hot from the oven or chilled with whipped cream.

2	ripe firm peaches, unpeeled
3	almond macaroons
pinch	sugar
1	egg yolk
1 tbsp. (45 mL)	unsalted butter, melted
	vanilla to taste
2 tbsp. (30 mL)	light rum *or* Marsala wine

Halve the peaches and remove the pits. Finely chop the macaroons. Mix with the sugar, egg yolk, a little of the butter and any pulp. Flavour with a little vanilla, if desired.

Fill the peach cavity with the mixture. Place the peach halves in a buttered baking dish. Drizzle with melted butter. Bake at 350° F(180° C) for 10–15 minutes, or until heated through. Sprinkle with rum or Marsala. Heat a further few minutes.

YUMMY PARFAIT

Make these three quick parfaits when dessert is a must but there just isn't time. A balloon-style wine goblet or crystal sherbet glass makes any one of them into party fare.

Peach Parfait

In a large wine goblet, place a round scoop of vanilla ice cream. Slice a peach on top. Add a little peach brandy (*or* other fruit and liqueur). **Makes 1**.

Banana Parfait

In a blender, mash a banana (*or* fruit of your choice). Add ice cream and a little milk. Blend until just mixed. Pour into a goblet and top with a sliced piece of the fruit. **Makes 1**.

Liqueur Parfait

In a blender, blend 1 pint (500 mL) ice cream with 1 oz. (30 mL) crème de menthe and 2 oz. (60 mL) of brandy. Pour into a goblet and serve with a straw. **Makes 2**.

CHAMPAGNE SPARKLERS

Champagne is a versatile mixer when used with fruit liqueurs. Try these ideas for brunch.

Raspberry Sparkler

1 tbsp. (15 mL)	raspberry liqueur *or* frozen raspberry concentrate
1 cup (250 mL)	sparkling wine

Add the raspberry liqueur to the wine in an attractive goblet. Serve well chilled. **Makes 1**.

Blackcurrant Sparkler

1 tbsp. (15 mL)	Cassis liqueur (blackcurrant liqueur)
1 cup (250 mL)	sparkling wine

Add the Cassis liqueur to the wine in an attractive goblet. Serve well chilled. **Makes 1**.

Orange Sparkler

1/2 cup (125 mL)	fresh orange juice
1/2 cup (125 mL)	sparkling wine

Add the orange juice to the wine in an attractive goblet. Serve well chilled. **Makes 1**.

WHITE WINE COOLER

This wine cooler is a little different from the coolers purchased at the liquor store. The brandy and liqueur give it a little extra pizazz! **Makes 1.**

3 oz. (90 mL)	white wine
3/4 oz. (22 mL)	brandy
3/4 oz. (22 mL)	curaçao *or* orange liqueur
	slice of orange
	soda, optional

Pour wine over crushed ice in a goblet or large wine glass. Add the brandy and curaçao. Stir gently. Garnish with orange slice. Add soda to fill the goblet, if desired.

LEMON SANGRIA

This drink is very refreshing on a hot summer's day. Enjoy it while preparing the barbeque for dinner. **Makes 5 cups (1.5 L).**

3 1/2 cups (875 mL)	dry white wine
3	unpeeled lemons, sliced
1	unpeeled orange, sliced
1	green apple, peeled, cored and cut into wedges
1/2 cup (125 mL)	cognac
4 tbsp. (60 mL)	sugar
1- 750 mL	bottle club soda, chilled
	ice cubes
	small bunches of green grapes

Combine all ingredients except soda, ice cubes and grapes in a large pitcher. Chill overnight. Just before serving, add soda and ice cubes. Stir lightly. Pour into tall glasses and add grapes as desired.

SANGRIA

Red sangria is more robust that the lemon version. I like to serve this one with Gazpacho for a delicious flavour treat.

1/2 cup (125 mL)	sugar
1 cup (250 mL)	water
1- 750 mL	bottle dry red wine
1/2 cup (125 mL)	brandy
1	sliced orange with peel
1	sliced lemon with peel
	ice cubes
	soda *or* 7-Up
	long peel from orange for garnish

Bring sugar and water to a boil. Reduce heat and simmer 5 minutes. Cool. Stir in wine and brandy. Add sliced fruit. Marinate overnight.

To serve, place ice cubes in tall glasses. Fill half full with the marinade. Top with soda or 7-Up. Garnish with orange peel.

To make a punch, pour all the marinade and fruit into a bowl. Add a large bottle of soda or 7-Up. Add a little orange juice and more red wine, if desired.

PERFECT LEMONADE

Nothing is more thirst quenching than lemonade and homemade lemonade is best of all! Make lots and keep it on hand in the refrigerator. **Makes 10 cups (2.5 L).**

1 cup (250 mL)	berry sugar
1 cup (250 mL)	water
1 1/3 cup (325 mL)	fresh lemon juice (about 6 lemons)
	zest of 2 lemons
2 qt. (2 L)	cold water *or* soda
	ice cubes
	lemon slices
	mint leaves

Combine the sugar and 1 cup (250 mL) water in a small pot. Bring to a boil. Reduce heat and simmer 5–6 minutes, stirring occasionally. Remove from heat and cool completely.

Combine sugar syrup, lemon juice and zest in a large pitcher or jar with a tightly fitting lid. The drink may be made ahead to this point and kept in the refrigerator for up to 7 days.

Just before serving, add cold water or soda. Stir vigorously. Fill tall glasses with ice cubes and pour lemonade over. Garnish with lemon slices and mint.

KEY WEST SUNSET

This East Coast sunset treat is just as delicious during a West Coast sunset. Serve with an antipasto tray as dinner readies in the oven. **Makes 1**.

	ice cubes
1 part	amaretto di saronno
2 parts	richly flavoured dark rum
1 part	freshly squeezed orange juice
1 tbsp. (15 mL)	lime juice, or to taste
	splash of club soda
	slice of fresh lime

Fill a large, stemmed balloon glass with ice cubes. Add the amaretto and dark rum, but do not stir. "Float" the orange juice on top of the liquors by pouring it slowly over the inverted bowl of a spoon.

Add the lime juice and a splash of chilled soda. Garnish with a single slice of fresh lime, slit halfway across and perched on the rim of the glass. The swirling burnt-orange liquid will bring to mind a deep-hued sunset.

PLANTER'S PUNCH

This mellow mixture can be kept for several days in the refrigerator. Serve with rum as indicated in the recipe. Or half fill a glass of ice cubes with the mixture and top up with soda. It also makes a nice base for a punch. **Makes 4.**

1 cup (250 mL)	freshly squeezed orange juice
1/2 cup (125 mL)	unsweetened pineapple juice
1/2 cup (125 mL)	guava juice
1 tsp. (5 mL)	freshly grated nutmeg
2 tsp. (10 mL)	angostura bitters
1 tbsp. (15 mL)	Sugar Syrup, recipe follows
2" (5 cm)	cinnamon stick
1	orange, thinly sliced
1	lemon, thinly sliced
	ice cubes
	pineapple and melon pieces
8 oz. (250 mL)	good golden rum
3	slices of orange for garnish

Combine the orange juice, pineapple juice, guava juice, nutmeg, bitters and Sugar Syrup in a 1 qt. (1 L) jar. Add the cinnamon stick, orange and lemon. Put the lid on tightly. Let stand in a cool place or in the refrigerator for about 5 days to let the flavours blend and ripen.

Half fill 4 tall tumblers with ice cubes and pieces of the fruit. Pour 2 oz. (90 mL) of rum into each tumbler. Fill with the punch mixture.

Serve with an orange slice impaled on the edge of each tumbler and a straw for sipping.

Sugar Syrup

When you use this syrup, you avoid the sediment and gritty drinks caused by undissolved sugar.

2 1/2 cups (625 mL)	berry sugar
1 cup (250 mL)	cold water

Put the sugar into a heavy 1 qt. (1 L) saucepan. Stir in the cold water. Heat to boiling, stirring occasionally. Boil the mixture vigorously until all the sugar is melted, about 4 minutes. Let the syrup cool, then bottle it. The syrup will keep indefinitely.

MARGUARITA

A favourite with Mexican dishes, try this variation with Gazpacho or Mexicana Bunwiches. Muy bueno! **Makes 1.**

1/2 oz. (15 mL)	lime juice
1/2 tsp. (2 mL)	sugar
1 1/2 oz. (45 mL)	tequila
	lime wedge
	salt

Shake lime juice, sugar and tequila well with cracked ice or purée in blender. Rub rim of a well-chilled cocktail glass with cut edge of lime wedge. Frost rim lightly with salt. Pour the drink into the frosted glass and serve.

SPANISH COFFEE

This coffee drink is rich enough to take the place of dessert. Serve on cold wintry evenings in front of a roaring fire. **Makes 1.**

1 oz. (30 mL)	brandy
1/2 oz. (15 mL)	rum
1 oz. (30 mL)	Kahlua
1/2 oz. (15 mL)	curaçao *or* orange liqueur
	hot coffee
	whipped cream
	cinnamon or nutmeg

Pour the brandy, rum, Kahlua and curaçao into a large mug. Fill with coffee and top with a dollop of whipped cream. Sprinkle with cinnamon or nutmeg.

INDEX